Copyright © Noah From 2017
Original Title: Känslostartk, Oavsett omständigheter
Graphic design and cover: Simeon Frohm
Editing and Proof reading: Anita Gold and Flora Brown
Illustration: Simeon Frohm
Contact: www.noahfrom.com
ISBN: 978-91-639-3970-9

Noah From

WONDERFEEL

No Matter The Circumstances

Wonderfeel - The ability to feel like we want no matter the circumstances

CONTENT

FOREWORD	6
INTRODUCTION - A Wonderful Life	8
CHAPTER 1. What are we really looking for? - The driving force of life	12
- What We Really Want	13
- Where Do Our Feelings Come From?	14
- Why Do We Feel Like We Do?	16
CHAPTER 2. Master Your Feelings – Three Decisions That Determines the Quality of Your Life	20
- The Winner of Life	22
The Force That is Shaping Your Life More Than Anything Else	25
CHAPTER 3. What Do Your Feelings Really Mean? - How To Understand and Communicate Our Feelings	38
- The Cause of Unwanted Feelings	39
- How Do Feelings Appear?	42
- Your Words Become Your Feelings	44
- Negative Feelings Do Not Exist	45
- "The Feel-Transformer" - How to Deal With Unwanted Feelings	48
CHAPTER 4. A Winning State – The Key to Your Inner Resources	55
- The Difference In People's Lives	57
- Master Your Life Experience	59
- Decide To Live A Wonderful Life	62
CHAPTER 5. The Root of All Good – Your Innermost Longing	67
- What Is Keeping You From Experiencing a Wonderful Life?	69
- To Find Heaven In Hell	72
- Life's Biggest Breakthrough	73
- Life's Biggest Challenge Becomes Life's Greatest Reward	74
BONUS - Our Ten Most Common Feelings - What They Mean and How We Can Deal With Them	78
EPILOGUE - Words of Inspiration	80
PS: - If You Want More	82

FOREWORD

I have always wondered how some people who seem to have "everything" can feel miserable, while others who have experienced hell on earth, manage to live a life in joy and gratitude? Regardless of where I find myself, at my workplace, on a family holiday, or in a rehab center working together with former child soldiers, I have asked myself the question: Is it possible to feel like we want no matter the circumstances?

Have you noticed that life seldom turns out as planned? There will always be unwanted suprises along the way. If we only feel happy when life turns out the way we want, we won´t be happy very often.

For a long time, I believed that my feelings were the direct result of circumstances and how other people treated me. When I felt bad, I blamed other people, my background, lack of time and money, the weather or the situation I was in. I lived a life where my emotional wellbeing was determined by the things happening to me. Many times I found myself overwhelmed by my own feelings, which in turn made me frustrated and exhausted.

The encounter with people who had all the reason to feel bad but didn't, would slowly but surely change the way I viewed my own feelings. Those were people who to a large extent had lost everything but still were able to live a life in harmony. They taught me that the only obstacle keeping me from feeling the way I wanted, was me and my understanding of how feelings actually work.

This book is the result of my own frustration, desperation, but also my yearning to use instead of being used by my own feelings. This book is full of ideas and practical approaches that (if we put them into use) can help us to take the first steps towards a wonderful life no matter the circumstances.

Someone once said "You teach best what you yourself is trying to learn" I believe that to be true. Therefore, everything written in this book are things I have learnt and am still trying to learn.

"If you will change, everything will change for you" -Jim Rohn

INTRODUCTION

A WONDERFUL LIFE

What defines a wonderful life for you? Is it a life spent with good friends, family, a great career, delicious food, great finances and fruitful relationships?

Have you ever met a person who had lots of money but still wasn't happy? Have you ever met a person who is surrounded by loving people, but still does not feel loved? Or a person who feels loved, but remains disappointed for not having the body, time, work or the success he or she wants?

If we would just take a moment to think, we would soon realize that a wonderful life does not come from achieved goals, good friends and family, more time, a dream partner, success in our career or more money. Surely, all of those things can be wonderful, but still, many people have achieved "everything" but still feel miserable and in some cases even decided to end their own lives. Yet, we manage to fool ourselves that it will be different for us. If we just can get all that we want, then, we will be happy.

> *"It's not where we live physically,*
> *but where we live internally that determines the quality of our lives."*
> – TONY ROBBINS

Have you thought about the fact that most of us tend to invest most of our time and energy in mastering the outside world? We work very hard to help others, improve our relationships, succeed at our workplace, manage our finances, careers and polish our looks. Busy creating a successful life on the outside, it is easy to forget that the quality of our life is not determined by things on the outside. The quality of our lives is determined by the quality of our inside. We carefully keep track of the latest news about the real estate market, the latest post on social media and the upcoming election, meanwhile many of us find ourselves unable to deal with feelings such as stress, anxiety and worry in a sustainable way.

Haven't we all experienced the power of feelings? The loneliness that eats us away, the worry that weighs us down, the anger that burns, the fear that feels like ice in our chest, the lust that blinds us, the joy that makes us free, and the passion that enables us to break through? The purpose of this book is to inspire you to open the door to perhaps one of life's greatest secrets, the art of mastering your inner world, namely the part of us called feelings.

I remember a man saying, "The quality of our lives reflects the quality of the feelings that we feel on a daily basis." Isn't that true? If we live a life in frustration, anger, disappointment, resentment, stress or self-pity, it wouldn't matter how many friends or how much money and professional success we have, everything would be in vain if we don't feel like we want to feel. However, if we live a life characterized by feelings like gratitude, passion, love, hunger, growth, hope, appreciation, and humility, it doesn't matter what you have or what is happening around you, you would still be able to live a wonderful life. So the question dealt with in this book is: Is it possible to live a wonderful life no matter the circumstances if we wanted to and in that case how?

Surely, a wonderful life differs in meaning depending on who you ask, but regardless of how we define a wonderful life, there is one thing in common; a wonderful life is a feeling. Would you agree? Or do you think it is possible to live a wonderful life while feeling miserable?

If we can agree that a wonderful life is a feeling or feelings, then we could define a wonderful life as the following: A life where we can feel the way we want, no matter the circumstances.

Many times unwanted feelings get in the way of what we want. Stress keeps us from relaxing, fear makes us afraid of trying, pride prevents intimacy in our relationships, performance anxiety keeps us from finishing, and disappointment robs us of hope. What if there is a way we can rule our feelings instead of being ruled by them?

For a long time I equated feelings to viruses. They would attack me when I was at my weakest. However, is that really the case? That feelings just come and go and that we are unable to do anything about it?

> "You cannot always control what happens on the outside of You,
> but You can always learn to control what happens on the inside of You."
> –WAYNE DYER

When we believe that our feelings are beyond our control, we start to avoid unwanted feelings by avoiding certain places, situations, and people. We all have our own way of dealing with unwanted feelings. Some people suppress their feelings in order not to hurt others or get hurt themselves. Other people scream and shout to let people know what they feel. Other times we overindulge in work, food, activities, medication, drugs or alcohol in the attempt to change the way we feel. A life where our feelings controls us will lead to a very limited life. But a life where we understand the function of our feelings and learn how to use them makes a wonderful life possible no matter the circumstances.

Just to be clear. I do not believe that the aim of life is to feel wonderful and happy all the time, emotional diversity is an important part of our life experience. We will all feel sad, afraid and overwhelmed sometimes, but knowing " how to" overcome such feelings constitutes an incredible asset. So, what if you can learn to use your feelings? What if your feelings instead of being a burden can become a source of power? What if you can move from worry to happiness in a heartbeat if you wanted to? What if your emotional life is like a muscle that you can work out and learn to use in order to live a life filled with the feelings you want?

> "Our fate is not ruled by high waves or strong wind,
> but by the set of our sail."
> –SAILOR

A life where we can feel the way we want, no matter the circumstances requires an ability to which makes that possible. That ability is something I have come to call " Wonderfeel" – The ability to feel the way we want no matter the circumstances. How to develop such an ability is what this book is all about.

This book can be viewed as an introduction to thoughts and ideas shared by thinkers, survivors, and successful people before us. Thoughts and ideas always have the power to transform our life experience if we choose to put them into practice. Change, or more accurately, improvement, always starts with a new thought and this book is full of such thoughts.

Most of what you will read in this book is like stolen riches, "stolen" from people I met and thinkers before me. I'm a bit like Robin Hood, in fact, I have been robbing the rich and would now like to give to anyone who dare to see themselves as "poor." After all, is there anything better than being poor in the sense that you are always open to new thoughts and ideas?

If not already, you will become acquainted with individuals such as Viktor Frankl but also less famous people such as refugees from Kosovo, genocide survivors from Rwanda and heroes from Stockholm city. This book is packed with people and wisdom that supports the belief that all of us, no matter the background or circumstances, already today, can design a life of emotional strength. A wonderfull life. A life where we can be Wonderfeel.

This book is also a "thank you" to all the people in my life. Thank you for letting me participate in your life and for your participation in mine. Your life journey has shaped my life journey, you have given me what I needed to become who I am today. I also would like to thank my mom and dad, for making this exciting life possible by putting me into the world. You mean a lot to me. In addition, I would like to aim a special thank you to philanthropist Jim Rohn and life strategist Tony Robbins, who have opened up the door to many of the thoughts, ideas, and approaches presented in this book.

CHAPTER 1

WHAT ARE WE REALLY LOOKING FOR?
- THE DRIVING FORCE OF LIFE

19 years old I moved to a new town in the south of Sweden. Excited and filled with expectation I thought to myself, get ready world here I come. For practical reasons my adventure started with me living with my aunt. My aunt and I got along just fine, but despite that, I was like many other 19-year-olds, preoccupied with the idea of freedom and independence. I wanted to stand on my own feet and feel like an adult. I wanted to become successful. Every night, I remember lying in my bed, staring up at my aunt's roof and thinking "If only I could get a good job, buy an apartment and get a car, then I would feel free and proud of myself."

Three months later, the alarm clock rang; I opened my eyes and stared up at the ceiling at my new apartment. When I sat up on the edge of the bed, I sighed deeply and came to myself. I shuddered at the thought of going to the job I now had, stressed out about refueling the car I had bought. This was not the freedom and independence I had yearned for. Despite the fact that I now had all I dreamed of just a few months earlier, I felt empty, restless, lonely, and confused.

Have you ever felt like something is missing? Like you want something more? Make a difference in the world, attain a greater career, buy a new house or perhaps have more money? If the answer is Yes, let me ask another question: What did you hope that would give you? Hypothetically speaking, if you got it, what would it have brought you?

One prominent characteristic for us as human beings is that we always want more. If you have a great job, then you want better health. If You have great health then you want deeper relationships etc. How many of us have ever bought something or finally got what we had so desperately longed for, just to discover that a short while after, found us longing for something else, something more? Many people manage to get everything they want, but seem to lack what they really need. The question remains: What are we really looking for, when we are constantly chasing after more? The secret lies in the answer to the next question: What do the following words have in common– Happiness, security, success, wealth, love, respect, self-confidence, strength, trust, power, ecstasy, disappointment, hatred, and joy? The common denominator for the above liste words is that they are all feelings.

Some of us are not ashamed to admit that we sometimes can be quite emotional. I, on the other hand, used to be a person who said, "I am not emotional, I'm rational." My approach to life was that you couldn't live life ruled by your feelings. I was the spry guy that tried to ignore unwanted feelings by saying stuff like, "Think positive." Now it is different for me. The turning point came when I was introduced to the idea below: *In everything we do, we are driven by feelings.* The first time I heard this, I was provoked. It sounded whimsical, "hippie" and abstract. But slowly and surely, the coin would drop. Let me explain.

WHAT WE REALLY WANT

When you strive or want something, the question is: do want it because of the object itself or because of the feeling you think it will give you? Think about it, is it really pieces of paper with dead men and women that make us yearn for money? Of course not! We want money because of the feelings we associate with money, freedom, power or community. Another example, is it really a metal piece engraved with their names that motivates a person to dedicate her life to win the Olympics? Of course not, it is the feelings that the person associates with the medal; fame, acknowledgment, and fulfillment. Likewise, when you go to the hairdresser to cut your hair, do you cut your hair because you want to trim the protein growth attached to your scalp, or do you cut it in order to feel nice, functional, stylish, fresh, sexy, or accepted? No matter what we want in life, we want it because of what we think it will make us feel. *Everything we do or want, we do or want because we believe it will change the way we feel.* Does it sound like an exaggeration? Maybe, but what if it is true. Irrespective of what you want, if you ask yourself the question "why do I want it?" enough times, you will discover that you want it because you believe it will change the way you feel.

For a long time I though "rational" people were the opposite to so called "emotional" people. That was before i realized that "rational" also is a feeling. All "rational" people don´t act in the same way and might aswell have different opinions regarding what the rational thing to do is. In the light of this we can understand that all we want or want to be, do we want or want to be because we believe it will make us feel in a certain way.

Pause for a minute and try this thought: Feelings are what motivates us, it is the force that determines whether we will act or not.

But wait a minute now, sometimes we do things even though they feel hard and uncomfortable. We go to the gym early in the morning, do gardening in the middle of pouring rain or confront our boss in public, are we really guided by our feelings then? Interesting thought, let me offer an alternative answer. One of the most satisfying feelings for us as human beings seem to be to act in alignment with who we want to be or who we believe we are. This feeling can get us to do things that in the moment make us feel uncomfortable in order to feel pleasure longterm. Our greatest reward seems to be staying consistent with our self-image, but more on that later.

WHERE DO OUR FEELINGS COME FROM?

If feelings are what decides what we do or won´t do, where do they come from? What makes us feel? Is it our partner, the weather, or Christmas? In the conversation about feelings, it´s easy to think that external factors are the source of our feelings. It is common to believe that events and people are what make us feel. We might think that it is our friendly neighbor, a vacation, good relationships, our job, possessions or a specific event can give us the feelings we want. We might think, when I accomplish that or when I get that, then I will feel at peace.

Outer circumstances have the potential to make it more or less easy to experience certain feelings. However, both you and I know that feelings are not attached to things, events or people. Otherwise, how is it possible that the same car can result in two completely different feelings for two different people? A dream ride for one person might be an embarrassing looking thing for another, so the feeling is not attached to the car. One day we like our shirt, the next day it is old and boring, so the feeling is not attached to the shirt. One moment, we are head over heels in love with our partner, the next moment we consider divorce, love doesn't either seem to be attached to a person.

But if it is not the things, people or events themselves that determine what we feel, what is it? It is how we think about the things that determines how we feel, more accurately: ***The meanings we assign to things, people, or events will determine our feelings about them.*** Let me explain with an example.

Tony gets angry with his wife Filippa because she comes home late and therefore misses dinner. When Filippa tells Tony the story about the car accident on her way home and how she had helped a person out of a car wreck, Tony's emotional state changes immediately. Tony's feelings were not caused by Filippa's late homecoming, but rather the meaning he had given her late homecoming. He was angry because he had given the situation a meaning that made him angry. As soon as he changed the meaning of the situation, he also experienced a change in his emotional reaction.

Throughout my childhood, I thought that feelings were something that happened to me. When somebody broke their word I was disappointed, when someone picked on me, I got angry, and when people did not understand me, I was irritated. I lived a life characterized by peaks of happiness just to fall down into valleys of worry and dissatisfaction. I realized that I had become a victim of external events and other people's behaviors. When reading a book by Kay Pollack, "Choosing Joy" I would come across a thought that had never crossed my mind before:

> *"Every thought I have about other people is a message to myself about myself."*
> -KAY POLLACK

The first time I read this I asked myself the question: Can it be that my feelings do not reflect reality but they reflect my perception of reality? What if my feelings are not the result of what is happening to me but the result of how I interpret the happenings?

Was I the one "making" myself angry, sad or irritated based on the meaning I gave certain events? This was for me a strange thought. The first time I heard that I was 100% responsible for all my feelings, I did not agree. What about all the terrible stuff that had happened to me? I felt attacked. But after a while it dawned on me, this might be the greatest news of my life. I might not be able to control the events of my life, but I can always control the way I responded to the event. If I was the key to a life full of wonderful feelings, I would never again have to wait for life or people to change or try to change them in order to feel the way I wanted, I could learn to control how I interpreted things and what they would mean to me.

Pause for a minute and ask yourself the question: Could it be that I am 100 percent responsible for all feelings that I have and that everything I feel comes down to the meanings I assign to situations and events?

WHY DO WE FEEL LIKE WE DO?

Having met with people who have gone through violence, abuse, and injustice but despite that, manage to live a life of joy and gratitude, I am convinced that *feelings are not the result of what happens to us but the result of how we choose to interpret that which is happening to us.*

The way we interpret situations, events, and other people is by assigning them different meanings. In short, the meanings we give an event or situation will determine how we will feel in that situation and event. For example, do you think it is human corpses, 40°C below zero, snow and rock that makes a person feel like a winner when reaching the top of Mount Everest (it might as well be a nasty grave site)? Of course not? A person who climbs the summit of Everest feels like a winner because he/she assigns a meaning that makes him/her feel like a winner.

We can learn to take 100 percent control over our feelings because we have 100 percent control over the meanings we assign. That, in turn, would mean that there isn't really anyone or anything that can make us feel anything, but our feelings are caused by meanings we create in our head and choose to give certain situations and events. Of course, circumstances can physically make it easier or harder for us to give meanings that make us feel good (physical pain and hunger for example), but it does not withhold the fact that it is we who decide what an event and situation will mean, and that meaning will become our experience.

> *"Nothing in life has any meaning except the meaning we give it."*
> - TONY ROBBINS

Our feelings can therefore be seen as information about the meanings we have given events, people, and their behaviors. So what causes so many of us to go through life and believe that we are helpless when it comes to feelings such as disappointment, frustration, anxiety, stress, and grief? How often do we not feel bad and think that our emotional state is beyond our control? We can say stuff like, "I'm having a bad day" or "I'm in a depressed place right now," as if feelings were something that suddenly jumps on us? Why do we think that external events and others people's behavior directly affects how we feel?

Pause for a second and ask yourself the following question: Did you as a child ever hear things like: "If you do that, mum is going to be upset" or "If you don't do as Daddy says, he'll get sad?". Already as children, we were programmed to believe that we are directly responsible for how people in our neighborhood feel. Indirectly, we were trained as children to believe that our actions have a direct impact on how another person feels. We learned to think in a way that made us victims of what is happening outside of us. This can be seen as one of the main reasons why we feel that external factors and other people are the cause of our feelings. This "victim" programing continues throughout our whole life by us saying things like: "My boss MAKES me so crazy. They don't understand me, and THAT MAKES me so incredibly stressed" or " My colleagues are thinking only about themselves IT MAKES me so irritated. "

Another reason why we blame our emotions on the circumstances and continue to hold other people responsible for our wellbeing is our driving force to maintain our self-image, who we believe ourselves to be. Would you like to see yourself as a frustrated, angry and selfish person? Not many people do, so every time we feel frustrated, angry and selfish, we simply let others bear the blame for our behavior– "it is not me, but the way they did that or said that causes me to behave like this." Instead of destroying our own self-image (which is the basis for our entire existence), we simply distort reality in order to create certainty and confidence in who we are.

> *"We don't see the world as it is, we see it as we are."*
> - ANAÏS NIN

Our whole life is based on our self-image, the ones we believe ourselves to be. Our relationships, our work, and our social lives are all based on who we see ourselves as. In an uncertain world that is constantly changing, we tend to count our self-image as the only constant in our lives and will do anything to protect it. Since we base our entire existence on our self-image, the preservation of it has become our strongest motivator. Our desire to preserve our self-image tend to make us blind to things we don't want to see in ourselves, things that could make us confused. Because what happens to a person who does not know who she is? Where does she belong? Where will she go? How will she tell good from bad? How will such a person be able to relate to other people, and above all, how will she be able to relate to herself?

Cracks in our self-image has consequences in all areas of life and therefore often perceived as one of life's most painful emotional experiences. It seems that we like to judge others rather than questioning the cornerstone of our life, our self-image. We end up protecting ourselves against unwanted feelings by making use of what is called the projections. For example, if we dislike a person, meanwhile our self-image says that it is not justified to do so, we solve the situation by imagining that they don't like us, then suddenly we have a justifiable reason to dismiss them. In this way, we don't have to feel unfair and nasty.

> *"Behind everything we find strange lies our own ignorance."*
> – NOAH FROM

In the light of all this, we all find ourselves at choice: one way of living is to live like I used to, with fingers crossed, hoping for a good day and avoiding painful situations and people. I was a victim of circumstances. Or, we could understand that we don't have to live a life in reaction, we don't have to let our feelings be automatic. We can acknowledge the fact that our feelings are the result of an inner process over which we can take control and learn to make use of.

The journey towards self-awareness, to challenge and update our self-image is a demanding process and an unfamiliar activity for many. We spend a lot of time working jobs, but very little time working on ourselves. Through a few simple approaches that follow in the next chapter, you will learn how to transform unwanted feelings to your strength and a fuel for life. The art of mastering your feelings is a prerequisite to improving not only our own emotional life, but our relationships and our professional life as well. Feelings can destroy us if we let them be our masters but can become a divine strength if we let them be our servants. Before we go any further in this book and talk about how we can transform and master our feelings, I would like to summarize what we have learnt so far.

TAKE AWAYS

Regardless of what we as humans strive for, it is really a quest to change the way we feel. All we want to achieve, accomplish or acquire is really a longing for what we believe it will make us feel.

It's common to blame our feelings on external circumstances, people and events, it is the result of a learned behavior and a way to preserve our self-image. We ascribe to others our own shortcomings to preserve the image of ourselves and thereby avoid feelings of insecurity and uncertainty.

It is not events or situations that make us feel as we do, but the meanings we assign to those events. Our feelings do not reflect, neither describe people or the world around us, but rather describe our way of seeing and interpreting the world and the people around us.

Since we can take 100 percent control over the meanings we assign situations and events, we can also take 100 percent control over our feelings.

CHAPTER 2

MASTER YOUR FEELINGS

- THREE DECISIONS THAT DETERMINE THE QUALITY OF OUR LIVES

When Elise was five years old, she only had one person whom she loved, her father. But he worked long days and was almost never home. However, her mom worked too, but not as much and when she wasn't working, she treated Elise in a hideous way. She used to lock her in a small dark closet with the reason that she was "ugly" and "stupid." Elise never dared to tell her father about what was going with her mother and even worse with the neighboring family. What started at five years of age would continue for many years to come.

While her parents were at work, Elise used to spend the afternoons at the home of a middle-aged couple without children of their own. Every day after lunch, the man would grab her by her tiny little wrist, lead her from the dining table into the bedroom next door and rape her. They always kept the door open so that the woman could sit and watch while the abuse was going on. When the man had finished, the woman would tell Elise in a threatening voice, "If you tell anyone about what we are doing to you, we'll kill you." Then she would give Elise a little brown bag with a few sweets in it and send her home.

Years passed and her parents separated. Her mother would soon find a new man; a man who did not make life any easier. He was constantly drunk and was always fighting. One day, he took out a shotgun and pressed it against her eleven-year-old little body. She remembered yelling to the man, "Please shoot me, I don't want to live." She survived. At the age of 14, she ran away from home. However, the misfortune was not over. Two years later, she became embroiled in a business where her body was sold to different men for money. She did not know then, that she had become what many would call a prostitute.

All of us will be exposed to situations and happenings where our potential and our ability are tested to its utmost limit. It seems that, it is in those situations that some people are crushed while others manage to grow, discover their potential, and get to know their true nature.

The outside world constantly told Elise that she was worthless. She was sexually abused, sold, beaten, and lived much of her life in emptiness and polydrug abuse. Elise is well acquainted with the feeling of having lost one's value as a human being and not to feel loved by anyone. You would think that she is entitled to hate the people who treated her this way. You cannot expect people like this to be happy. Frankly speaking, she does have every right to feel hatred, anger and bitterness. I agree with that to a 100 percent. The remarkable thing with Elise is that she doesn't.

Instead of giving the events of her life meanings that resulted in feelings of hatred, fear, and worry, Elise is a living proof that no matter what circumstance, we can always choose meanings that will empower us. Today Elise is living a life loving people and loving life. Instead of hating the people who did her so wrong, she has managed to forgive them. Elise has managed to give the events of her life a meaning that converted all the bad things that she went through to a force that today fuels her to help and rescue other women trapped in the sex trade. Elise's background and problems have made her a key to other people who otherwise would have been locked up in the prison of hopelessness.

Image: Simeon Frohm

Cuts are what makes a key. The hardship we experience turns us into keys with which we can open the door to the life we are destined to live.

If you've ever met Elise Lindqvist (The Angel on Malmskillnadsgatan), you notice a glow of power, warmth, and joy. She says, "It is by helping and giving that I can heal and keep growing." Elise describes that an encounter with Jesus was the turning point, which enabled her to stop running away from the pain of her past. She was given a new identity. Now, this is no "Jesus book" in that sense, but Elise's story is interesting whether you believe in God or not. Elise talks about an encounter with a forgiveness that made it possible for her to forgive herself and about an unconditional love that allowed her to start loving herself and others. Elise's story is not a story about a woman who has learned to think positively, forget or suppress her painful feelings. Elise's story is that of a woman who chose not to be a victim of circumstances, but to take responsibility for her own life and feelings. When she changed on the inside, everything changed on the outside for her.

THE WINNER OF LIFE

In my life, I have had the honor to spend time and work along with heroes like Elise. A hero is someone who has experienced enormous injustice and gone through what many would call hell on earth, but who has come out on the other side to inspire and encourage other people. We all have people like that in our lives. These heroes can teach us something:

> "It is not the event that determines the turn out of our lives, but what we choose to do with that event. It is not what we have that determines the quality of our lives, but what we choose to do with what we have."
> - JIM ROHN

We've all seen or heard examples of people who seem to have it all- success, family, houses, money, and fame, but still chose to commit suicide. These are people that from the outside often are regarded as the winners of life. They seem to be living a life worth living, but in the end, those were the people who thought life was so unbearable that they chose to end it themselves. It clearly shows that "success" without fulfillment is the ultimate failure, to have everything but still feel like something is missing; to "succeed" but still not feel happy.

Alongside those tragic life stories, we hear the stories about people as Elise, who despite a difficult, painful, and broken past, managed to find meaning, strength, and joy. They seem to have figured out a way to defy, defeat, and overcome the darkness of despair. They are people who manage to turn a traumatic childhood to a life of gratitude and abundance and a life of unhappiness to a life of success. Despite their background, they manage to become life's winners. So, what determines if a person will become a winner of life or loser?

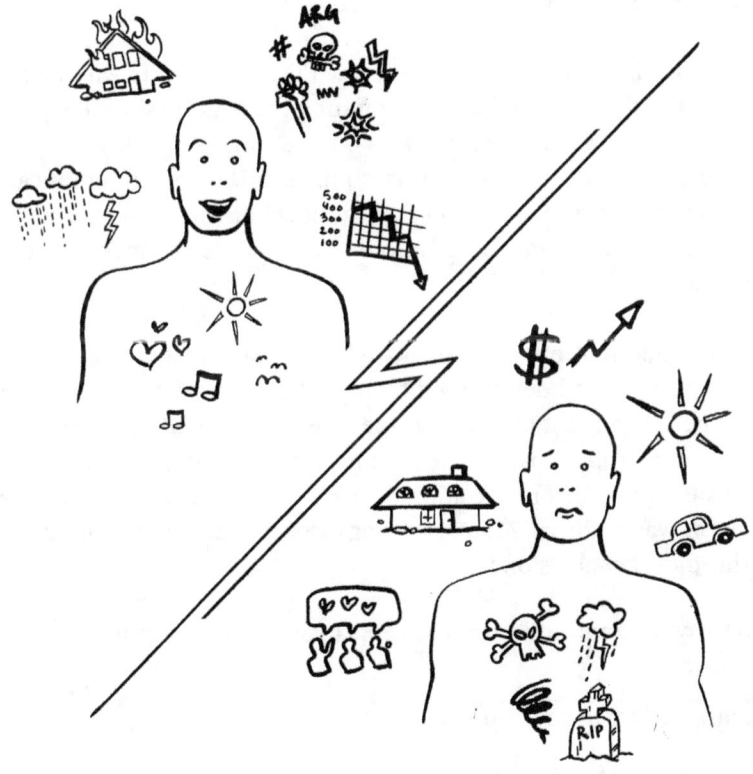

Image: Simeon Frohm

It is not the outside that determines how we feel, but the inside.

What makes Elise a winner in my book is a matter of focus. Winners are people who have plenty of reason to focus on all the pain they have experienced in their life. They have every reason to give their life the meaning of "game over". Winners are people who have every reason to throw in the towel, feel sorry for themselves, but instead, they do the opposite. Winners are people who, regardless of circumstances or resources, choose a meaning that allows them to love others. A person without arms or legs, hearing or vision, someone who lost her family or endured pain still finds a way to contribute to other people's hope, joy, and well-being. Winners are those who have developed a belief system that empowers them and the people around them. Winners do not act according to how they think life "should be," but learn how life works and act in accordance with that. They are the ones teaching us that it is not the external event that limits us, but rather how we deal with the event.

To master our inner world is not easy, ask Elise. It all starts with a strong enough reason to do it and the understanding that it is possible. People like Elise teach us that the crucial factor, if we are to master our inner world and be able to thrive regardless of circumstances, is the communication we conduct with ourselves. In other words, it is not what happens but how we communicate the happenings to ourselves that determines the quality of our lives.

When I realized that my emotional wellbeing was independent of external circumstances and determined by my own self-communication I had a hard time accepting it at first. But the more I read, and the more time I spent with heroes like Elise, single parents, former child soldiers, and people who survived the concentration camps, I started to see that self-communication was a unifying factor amongst successful people regardless of area. The logical conclusion is:

1. The way we communicate life's events to ourselves determines how we feel.
2. Feelings move us to action.
3. The way we act determines our results.
4. Our results become our lives.

In other words: The quality of our lives is the quality of our communication, first and foremost the communication with ourselves.

The thought of being the one responsible for our own feelings through our self-communication make some people feel uncomfortable. We don't like the thought of being responsible for the painful feelings we have. Other people read this and experience a feeling of hope. If our feelings depend on our self-communication, then we can learn to change our emotional experience anywhere and at any time. Our well-being does not have to be dependent on circumstances. In other words, if we don't like how we feel in any area of our lives, it just means that it's time to start changing the way we communicate life to ourselves in that area. How?

THE FORCE THAT IS SHAPING YOUR LIFE MORE THAN ANYTHING ELSE

People like Elise teach us that if there was a single force shaping our lives more than anything else, it is the force of decision making. Our self-communication consists of decisions and our decisions determine our feelings. Everything we feel is the result of the decisions we make. Whatever circumstances, background or resources, we all have the power to make three decisions. We make these three decisions every day, in every situation and every moment. Whether we are aware of them or not, these three decisions shape our lives and our experiences of life more than anything else. *The first decision* we make in each situation is:

What we choose to FOCUS on

In every moment of our lives and in every situation, we decide what we're going to focus on. What we choose to focus on will determine what we think about and where our energy will be invested, "Where your focus goes your energy flows." In every situation, we consciously or unconsciously ask ourselves the question, "What should I focus on?" No matter if it is a walk around town, a conversation with a friend or in the midst of stock market hysteria. In every situation, we choose what to focus on.

Our brain is designed to help us survive. It is in the nature of our brain to constantly be focusing on and looking for things that can hurt and harm us. Through exaggerating the threat, the brain aims to push us towards action. Throughout history, this defense mechanism has served us well and helped us survive both lions and bears. But, since wild animals are no longer a threat to most of us, our brain is now focusing on "threats" like "What will other people think of me?" "Do I have what it takes?" and "What if I fail?". If we don´t take charge of our focus and let this primitive defense mechanism automatically run us, we will be in trouble and our life experience will be characterized by stress and anxiety. If we instead start to take charge of our focus, we will also be able to take charge of our feelings. This is the first step towards a life where we use our feelings instead of being used by them.

Focus is what makes the difference. Our brain processes millions of bits of information every second. While you are reading this, you can be focusing on your hand, your phone, the feel of your clothes against your skin or the smell in the room you're in. If we were to process all gathered information with our conscious mind, it would cause an overload. Therefore, the brain must continuously make a selection of all information. Our focus filters all information gathered by our senses. We use mainly two types of focus:

· Bottom-up focus – Is when we let external circumstances decide what we focus on and react to whatever happens around us.

· Top-down focus – Is when we consciously take charge and decide what to focus on.

In other words, we can let our focus become an automatic process and focus on whatever happens in our lives or we can learn to consciously take control and focus on what we want more of, so that our energy flows in that direction. The receipt on a person owning her focus is when she stops asking questions like "Why does this happen to me?" and starts asking "What do I want to happen?"

Much of the emotional disorder in todays society is caused by lost focus. Most of us do not own our own focus. We have become animals of reaction and allow external events to constantly steal our focus. We are constantly distracted by our phones, emails, a thousand media channels, the demands of our job and school. We want to help our family, become financially successful, make a difference in the world and be the best looking person at the bar. At the same time we have to deal with terrorism and the world economy. We have lost focus and it comes with a price.

Besides my driver's license, the closest thing I've come to Autosport is bumper cars at the amusement park. When listening to a man who practiced STCC and NASCAR, I learned that one of the most crucial things to learn is to handle situations when the car loses traction and starts skidding. As you can understand, a skid while driving in 200 km/h is an entirely different story than me driving a turquoise funfair-car risking running into a rubber rim at 10 km/h. This is life on the line.

To learn how to recover from a skid, the racing trainer creates a crash-simulation. In order to simulate a crash, the trainer uses a "Skid car" (Swedish invention). The new driver is at the wheel, and the coach sits in the passenger seat. The special feature of a skid car is that the coach at any time can be pushing a button to raise any tire from the ground, thereby creating a situation of total chaos and put the car in a spin.

At the beginning of the crash simulation, the new driver is usually prepared, but as speed increases, the driver starts focusing on the technical execution of driving, that's when the trainer suddenly pushes the button that puts the car in a spin. When this happens, the most common reaction among new drivers is to focus on everything he/she is afraid of crashing into and starts thinking, *"Don't crash, don't crash"*. If the new driver does not listen to the instructions given by the trainer, the trainer will take his hand and force the new driver's head to focus in the direction, in which he or she wants to go. And sure enough, the tires soon find grip, and the car starts steering towards the right direction again. The lesson learned by the new driver is: Always FOCUS on where you want to go and not on what you're afraid of crashing into.

Our focus tends to determine our steering. Throughout the race training, the new driver repeatedly insists on watching in the direction where he or she is about to crash, while the coach continues to force the new driver to focus in the aspired direction. Finally, the new driver gets it. When the new driver shifts focus, a shift in direction takes place almost automatically. Gravity will make the car find grip regardless of road condition, and a crash can be avoided. It all starts with a shift in focus.

However, will shift of focus guarantee that we will never crash? Of course not. Both you and I together with the racing coach knows that when we learn how to control our focus and start changing direction, there will always be a risk of crashing. At the same time, the truth remains that if we focus on what we are afraid of and don't want to crash into, it is certain that we will get more of that. It is by finding an empowering focus that we, like the racing driver, has the best chance to regain control, regain grip and get back on track.

All of us understand that a car's change of direction will not be immediate. Due to the accumulated speed, there is something we call "lag-time." Lag-time denotes the delay between the shift and the effect. Still, regardless of the lag-time, the coach knows that the most crucial moment is the driver's shift of focus. Changed focus is the trigger of change in direction.

You can easily test this principle yourself by either locating the closest racing club or you can do like I did. I tried the same principle using my bicycle. I cycled with high speed into a tight curve and forced myself to focus only on the exit of the curve. If you try it, you will experience something almost magical.

What if the same principle is applicable in our emotional life? Just like racing, life seems to be less about living flawlessly and more about our ability to recover when we have started skidding. Both you and I know that challanges will occur. As soon as we change our focus in life, life's change of direction is initiated. At the same time, it is good to remember the lesson of lag-time. Usually, when we decide to make a change in our lives, we have to consider the speed we have built up in a certain direction. Depending on the speed, it will take a while before the tires regain traction and the change to be noticeable. Remember, it's not the tires (material resources) that are the determining factor if the car comes back on track. Regardless of the quality of your tires or even if the ground is icy, the car will in time turn around, if you just change your focus and steer in that direction.

Do you recognize this from your own life? Have you ever heard yourself say, "Hey, I've actually been trying this for two months now, but I still see no results." Lag-time my friend. If you have lived in a certain way for 25 years, you have built up an awful speed in that direction and the higher speed you have, the longer the lag-time. But the fact remains, as soon as you make a shift in focus and direction, you will in time regain grip, even on ice.

Just like the new driver's initial reaction, we all have a tendency to focus on the scary wall and think "Don't crash, don't crash." Many of us tend to focus on what we are afraid of and we get caught up in the so-called "crash thoughts" like, "*What if I decide to do this, but fail to follow through?*" "*What if this relationship ends with both of us getting hurt?*" "*What will happen if I don't manage to put this project together?*" or "*What happens if people never see how talented I am?*" What you choose to focus on, you will always get more of. In other words: What you focus on will become your emotional experience.

> *"Seek and you will find"*
> – MATHEW 7:7

Whatever we seek, we will find, and the key is: We are the ones deciding what to look for. You are like a camera. You decide what to focus on and what to zoom in on. If we focus on what is wrong with a person or in a situation, we will find lots of errors. If we instead focus on what is good even in a difficult situation, we will find plenty of good. To focus on everything we don´t have or cannot control is the perfect strategy in order to experience pain in life. To focus on what we fear will make us more afraid, while focusing more on what makes us safe will reinforce the feeling of being safe. The key is to focus and seek in earnest. This is as theoretically sustainable as practical. Try the bicycle exercise again, bike with high speed into a curve and focus on everything you don't want to crash into. You will be forced to slow down or you will crash. You decide to a 100 percent what to focus on. The best thing you can do is to find an empowering focus that builds you up and drives you towards your aspired direction

If you're anything like me, you might think, "Ok, this sounds good and all, but it is not always easy to just shift my focus, how do I find a strengthening focus when I get caught up in a spin?" Good question.

In every situation, no matter what happens we can always choose what to focus on. The way we decide what to focus on is by consciously or unconsciously asking ourselves questions. Actually, our entire thinking process consists out of asking and answering questions, for example, "Am I hungry? Is this love? What should I do now?" Whatever question we ask ourselves, our brain will come up with an answer to.

If we ask ourselves unproductive and poor questions, our brain will generate a focus that will disempower us and make us weaker instead of stronger. Poor questions generate poor answers and therefore a poor focus, which will make us poor. For instance, it is not unusual for people who expected a pay-raise but did not get it to unconsciously start asking themselves questions like: Doesn´t my boss value me? Since our brain is the world's fastest machine, it will instantly come up with an answer. If we ask a question like the above, our brain might come up with a reply like: "She is probably thinking of firing me." What will such an answer do to us, empower or disempower us? Surely it will lead to a spiral of disempowering and negative thought patterns. All of a sudden, because of a poorly asked question, we spend the next three months in a "reality" where we feel like we are on the verge of being fired. Walking on eg shells and feeling nervous we start to go "the safe way" rather than being brave and creative. If we get ideas, we hesitate to share them and keep a low profile instead of contributing. Our confidence in relationship with our boss gets worse and we become like a pink mouse. Indeed, three months later, we get called up to the boss' office and she says, "I'm terribly sorry, but the company has to lay off all pink mice." In such situation, the easiest thing to do is to blame the cold-hearted boss, the work environment or other external factors, when the crash, in fact, was caused by questions we asked ourselves unconsciously. Usually, it is the questions we ask ourselves that generate a focus that drives us right into the wall we try to avoid.

What could have been a more empowering way to act in the same situation? Let us look at the situation again. We get the same information regarding the declined pay raise. Our learned behavior and the initial reaction is still that we start by asking a question like, "Doesn't my boss value me?" But this time, instead of starting to think crash thoughts, we stop and ask ourselves a better question. We know that a better question leads to a better focus, so we ask ourselves, "What is great about this?" or "What can I learn from this?" It might sound a bit absurd of course, but it will make our brain come up with a more creative response, a response like, "Hmm, interesting. My boss seems to view a pay raise as an expense rather than an investment. Maybe I can change that by providing more value than I'm currently doing." Do you think such a response could get us to start thinking a bit more creative? Of course! In the beginning, we may not know how we could contribute to added value, but we keep on asking ourselves empowering and creative questions which will help us figure it out.

> "Ask and you shall receive, so make sure to ask intelligently."
> - JIM ROHN

Solutions come when we ask solution-oriented questions. So over the next three months, we decide to focus on the challenges of the company and ask ourselves, "What can I do here to contribute to the solution?" To make us part of a solution will make us feel like we are playing a central role in the company. Unlike the previous example, three months later without being called to the boss' office, we decide to take the initiative and present an intelligent, cost-effective, practical and feasible plan on how to solve the challenge, which the boss herself presented at the latest board meeting. Would this scenario increase our chances to get the pay raise? More importantly, would this way of thinking and acting cultivate our ability to handle difficult situations better? Of course.

THE PAST	THE PRESENT	THE FUTURE
GUILT	ACTION	WORRY / ANXIETY

Image: Simeon From

Do we have to ask productive questions even when we have feelings such as worry and sorrow? You don't have to. The goal is not to, never have feelings such as worry and sorrow, but rather to develop the ability to get out of such feelings if you want to. Unwanted feelings cease to be insuperable problems when we understand that they are the result of our focus. The first step to experience the feelings we want is therefore to change our focus. This is different from positive thinking. There is nothing wrong with positive thinking, but to run around in your garden chanting, "There are no weeds, there are no weeds," won't get rid of the weeds. I believe in intelligence, in other words, to understand how things work and do it that way. An intelligent person who got weeds in his garden does not have to think positively but understand that the key to a healthy garden is to acknowledge the weeds, pull them out, and replace them with fruit bearing plants. In the same way, can we replace disempowering questions with questions that will empower us. A wonderful life prerequisite is finding an empowering focus in every situation, that all starts with asking better questions.

What do you prefer to focus on?

- Your past – Things from our past that you can't do anything about since they already happened. My experience is that it often results in guilt.

- The future – Something we can't control. My experience is that an exaggerated future focus tends to cause concern and anxiety which means that we run the risk of becoming incapacitated.

- The Present – The only thing that we can change and influence. By focusing on something we can do in the present moment, we can build a life that will result in a brighter future.

> *"Where focus goes, energy flows"*
> – TONY ROBBINS

We always focus on something. Stop for a moment and think of a situation that stresses you. Do it now! Are you doing it? Good! Then consider the following questions: What do you focus on in that situation? Do you focus on what you don't have or what you do have? What you can control or what you can't control? All the good things or all the terrible things that can happen?

Whenever a person focuses on what is missing, what you cannot control or all the terrible things that might happen or has happened, it usually results in feelings of emptiness, frustration, and worry. If we do not learn to own our focus, circumstances will start owning us. Now do the opposite and think of a situation where you felt really good. Do it now. Consider then the following questions: What did you focus on in that situation?

The good news is that we can change our focus in an instant, it just takes practice. Just as we did when we learned how to tie our shoes. Most of us are experts on tying shoes today, but it took an everyday practice. To direct our focus is like training a muscle, it will develop through constant training. The key to an empowering focus no matter the circumstance is, an every day practice. The more often we train ourselves to focus on; all that we have and are grateful for, everything that is possible and everything we can do, the easier it will become. When we start to see the results of an empowering focus, we will become addicted. Remember, it is not the circumstances that need to change in order for us to feel like we want, it is when our focus changes that our experience of the world will change. **The second decision** that we always have the power to take is…

The MEANING we assign

In each and every situation, we also possess the power to decide what things MEAN. The meanings we choose to give certain events and situations determine how we feel and where we spend our life emotionally.

Take a minute and answer the following questions: Do you know anybody who has lots of money but isn't especially happy? Do you know someone who has very little money but is very happy? Do you know anyone who dislikes snow? Do you know anyone who loves snow? What is the difference? The difference is the meanings they give. Meanings are the difference between a person who seems to have everything but who is bitter and disappointed and a person who has gone through hell and still manages to be grateful and loving.

Is it possible for a person who by definition is rich communicate to herself a meaning that makes her feel poor? Of course. And, for one person, snow means cold darkness while for another snow can mean an opportunity to get together with friends, warm each other up, go skiing, and drinking hot chocolate. Again, it is not the event itself that determines how we feel, but the meanings we give the event. What's controlling people's experiences and feelings in a situation is not the situation itself but the meaning they assign to the situation. As we said before, nothing in life has any meaning except the meaning we choose to give it.

For instance, what meaning do you think an overweight person give the gym? Probably a meaning that makes him or her feel uninspired to go there. While coaching overweight people, I noticed that they usually give the gym meanings such as "waste of time," "stress" and "a place for snobs" while fit people assign the gym meanings such as "opportunity," "life investment" and "power station" The same gym, different meanings. The same gym different feelings, different feelings result in different behaviors, different behaviors result in different results, different results become different lives. It all comes down to the meanings we give.

In a relationship for example, would the meaning "this is the end for us" make us act and feel differently than if we gave the same relationship the meaning, "this is the start of something new?" If we got fired or our business went "belly up," would the meaning, "I will never take any risks again" make us feel and act differently than if we gave the same situation the meaning, "This happened so that I could grow as a person and become a more experienced businessman?" I'm not saying that one is right and the other is wrong, I'm just saying that we always have the choice to give a meaning that either empowers us or disempowers us. The meaning we give either limits us or creates possibilities.

A while ago, I read an article about a man named Mike Coots. Mike was a surfer from Hawaii and was attacked by a shark that bit his leg off. The story of Mike Coots who met jaws of death and had to pay with his leg sounds like a dreadful story. The fascinating thing about Mike is that after the initial pain and stay at the hospital, he developed a passion for saving sharks. The passion evolved and today he is fighting against shark "finning" and has run several campaigns against the sale of shark fins.

Most people would think that having your leg bitten off by a shark, would be a legitimate reason to become bitter and disappointed to say the least. Why? Evidently, because he had lost his leg and maybe even his future as a surfer. The interesting thing about Mike was the meaning he chose to give the situation. He said in the interview that it was not the shark's fault "... he just happened to be in the wrong place at the wrong time." Furthermore, he understood that the incident would probably make people want to clear the nearby waters from sharks. His accident could be the cause of an entire shark population being wiped out, but he had the power to stop it. The final meaning he gave the situation was that he had the power to save an entire shark population. Imagine, a situation that could have meant the end meant the beginning of a life full of meaning and purpose for Mike.

If the same thing had happened to you and I, what MEANING would we have given the experience? That we now would be handicapped for the rest of our lives, that we never could be seen as sexy again or that life is unfair? I'm not saying it is always easy to choose an empowering meaning, but that does not make it less true that we in any given situation have the power to do it. Mike decided to give a situation that could have meant trauma and loss, a MEANING that instead generated a life mission. He teaches us that the choice of MEANING lies with us.

> "It is not the events of life that make us feel like we do,
> it is the meanings we attach to those events."
> - TONY ROBBINS

Think about it, is it really wet skin tissue that makes us want to kiss someone? No, of course not, then kissing a pig would have been equally pleasurable. The reason we want to kiss a person is because we have given kissing that person a particular meaning that results in passion, joy, and love. It's not the kiss itself, but what we associate the kiss with. When we feel butterflies in the stomach, it is because we have certain rules that say, "When I kiss someone who looks a certain way, smells a certain way, speak, think and relate to me in a certain way, then it means that I'm in love." At that moment, when we decide that it is ok to feel pleasure, a bunch of nerve signals is sent to the brain, which results in a physiological change in our face, our body, and the way we breathe changes. A biochemical change takes place in our entire nervous system (every cell of our body), which results in a certain physiological state. It is this state we have the power to give whatever meaning we like. The meanings we give our physiological state becomes our feelings, and our feelings become our experiences. I will elaborate on this in chapter four.

When we understand that it is the meanings we assign that determines the way we feel, we can start changing our emotional experiences and encounters with people. Our experience will change when our meaning changes. When we experience disappointment, sorrow, anger or frustration we can stop and ask ourselves: what meaning did I assign to this certain event? Am I giving this situation a meaning, which serves me, or a meaning, which makes me weak? In the case of Mike Coots, could it be that some people actually see him as a gimp and a crippled loser? Of course. However, will such a meaning help Mike to live a rich and fulfilling life? Absolutely not.

We can't always control what happens to us, but we can always, take 100 percent control of what happens inside of us, that is, how we feel. We do this by choosing to FOCUS on what we want more of and giving events and situations empowering MEANINGS.

The third decision that we also have absolute control over is...

<u>What we choose to DO</u>

What we choose to do in situations often reveals the focus we have and what meanings we give the situation. Since we can control our focus and the meanings we choose to give, it becomes clear that it is possible to control our actions. Our actions are the result of our focus and our assigned meanings.

A few years ago, my grandmother passed on and the day came when it was time for the funeral. Family came from far to participate in the funeral and say their goodbyes to our beloved mother, grandmother, and friend. The ceremony was solemn and beautiful, and the room was filled with admiration and respect for life's fragility. After the priest had shared a few memorable words from the Bible, it was time for a song that grandma had wished to be sung at her funeral. When the brickle voice started to echo between the thick stone walls of the chapel, none of us could hold it back anymore. We all felt how our throats began to thicken and tears started crawling down. In respect, I sat with my head bowed. At the end of the song, I lifted my eyes and looked around. I saw my mother, beautiful in her black skirt and fine blazer with tears coming down her cheeks. On the same row further away, sat my aunt and my sister, struggling against the tears and mourning over the fact that Grandma was not among us anymore. While I let my gaze sweep across the people in the chapel, I got stuck on a young man who sat and smiled. It was my brother. With a smile from ear to ear and eyes that glimmered he looked as if he did not have a care in the world, even less concerned about our grandmother's passing and the fact that she had left us. After the ceremony and burial, he came up to me and said, "Noah, wasn't it beautiful?"

After speaking with my brother, I understood what had made him smile in such situation. While the majority of us focused on losing one of our most precious family members, he focused on all the beautiful moments they had together and everything that he had learned from her. While we gave grandmother's death, the meaning that we would never see her again, my brother chose the meaning that it was a chance for the family to draw close and tighten the family bonds. We experienced it as a moment of sadness and loss; my brother chose differently. He chose to see it as a chance to support, comfort, love, and grow as a person. So he did. He is a practical example of the fact that after choosing what to focus on and assigning an empowering meaning, we always have the choice to decide what to DO.

When winter arrives we all have the choice to freeze to death or to come together and warm eachother up. After we have chosen our focus, assigned a meaning, we all have the choice to decide what to DO.

In the same way and not so long ago a young man in my church died. Only 25 years old David fought cancer to his last breath. On the evening of his passing, a memorial service was held. Approximately 50 church members gathered to honor the memory of a young, enterprising joy. I went into the Church and sat down. In the front of the chapel candles were glittering and it lit up the memorial photo of David. He seemed so untouched by life, so unsuspecting and excited.

After a while, I noticed a man on the other side of the room. Like me, he sat alone, so I decided to go and sit next to him. After having introduced myself and we both described how we knew David, the man began to boil over. "How could God do this? How could life be so cruel? Why would God choose to end the life of a young man this early?" His sadness was evident, and his eyes were full of disappointment. I turned my eyes to the photograph and looked at the picture of David again. So happy and full of strength.

Around us sat people who barely knew each other and hugged. People who probably never had exchanged words talked about the meaning of life. Then it came to me, David had given us one of life's greatest gifts, something that a priest could never express in words; perspective. Realizing that nothing we have is to be taken for granted. That all we have is our stewardship. No Sunday service in the world could have given us what David gave us. I prayed a silent prayer for David, his family, and at the same time, I felt so grateful for my own life. David's death may have been a tragic event in many ways, but I'm sure if we had asked David today what he wanted his death to mean, it would not be pain and despair, but rather a reminder of life's fragility and a reminder to steward all that we have been given and live life to the fullest, as if today was the last.

Death, accidents, diseases, and sudden losses are often situations where we find it difficult to understand why it happens. The difference between people who "go under" and people who make it through is not the happening itself but the way they choose to deal with the happening. Hard times is not reserved for special people; we will all have our moments of trial, situations where it feels as if everything comes crashing down. The question is: what will we choose to do with it? Will we isolate ourselves from other people, stop believing or will we take the chance to discover the depth of life, explore our relationships, and develop faith in the future. One way will lead to us slowly but surely fade away while the other will allow us to explore our potential and experience the greatness of life.

TAKEAWAYS

The quality of your life is the quality of three decisions you consciously or unconsciously make at every moment. Decisions regarding what to focus on, what it means and what to do. These three decisions will determine how we feel.

Medication might help a person who feels unwanted stress or depression to numb the pain and provide short-term relief, but the question is: Will it be able to help longterm if the person retains a destructive focus and continues to give meanings of hopelessness?

Successful people in all areas of life have learned that it is not what happens in our lives that determine how we feel, but what we do with it, more specifically, what we do with our focus, meanings, and actions.

CHAPTER 3

WHAT DO YOUR FEELINGS REALLY MEAN?

HOW TO UNDERSTAND AND COMMUNICATE OUR FEELINGS

The clock struck 8:00 pm and the majestic sun of Africa are slowly making its way down the velvet sky. Even though the day was steaming hot, the entry of the rainy season has started to cool the air. I found myself in Nyanza, one of Kenya's most scenic provinces, but also one of the poorest. After a hard day's work, I felt (for the first time in four months) a little tired and worn out. With joints aching and a shy headache knocking at my head, I turned to aspirin for help, which shortly made me feel a bit better. Nevertheless, I decided to go to bed. I tightened the mosquito net around my bed and soon fell asleep.

After just an hour or so, I woke up in soaking wet sheets. The fever was raging. I was hot like an oven and had an unbearable headache. In a feverish daze, I got up trying to make my way into the kitchen. I had a drink and took another aspirin. The cold stone floor felt freezing against my roasting feet soles while wobbling through the darkness toward the water container in the kitchen. Once in the kitchen, I started to freeze like never before. The sweat on my body turned into ice water streaming down along my spine. I stumbled my way back to the bed. Equipped with an extra blanket and a warm sweater, I crawled back into the wet sheets. The aspirin soon began to kick in, and I fell asleep. The night turned out to be long and anxious, and I was tossed between the unbearable heat of Hades and the biting cold of the North Pole. Aspirin helped me relieve most of the pain.

Morning finally came, and I woke up with the angelic song of birds singing outside the window. My state was completely changed. I felt well again and became grateful that it was over. What a night, I thought to myself unaware of the fact that the next night would be worse. Battling the hallucinations and fighting the steady grip of fever I used the only weapon I could think of, aspirin.

The following day, I decided to visit a clinic in the area. It turned out that I had malaria. After travelling to another nearby village for further testing, they confirmed my malaria diagnosis. After one more night commuting between ice and fire, I received treatment and was soon back on my feet.

Malaria doesn't have to be dangerous. Normally the patient gets well as soon as she receives treatment. The danger occurs when you treat the symptoms and not the cause. Only treating the symptoms enables malaria to grow and worst case scenario causes death. My rescue was finding out the cause of the symptoms, until then I was treating the symptoms. The doctors at the hospital told me that all the aspirins I had used to endure the pain had covered the real issue and could have caused me my life. The "medicine" I had used to reduce the pain had allowed the disease to thrive within me.

Just as we can't get well from malaria by treating the fever and headache, we cannot achieve long term well-being as long as we believe our feelings to be the problem. Just as fever and headaches are not the reason we get sick, our feelings are not the reason we feel bad. Our feelings are never the cause, they are just the symptoms of the cause. The key to become wonderfeel and emotionally fit is to understand what is causing our feelings and take control over that process.

THE CAUSE OF UNWANTED FEELINGS

Viktor Frankl was the psychiatrist who survived the hell fires of Auschwitz. In his book, "Man´s search for meaning," he brings to the fore the importance of our internal communication. His stories from Auschwitz, portrays some of his fellow prisoners, some of which started to shut down emotionally only to slowly but surely assume dead states and eventually would die physically as well. At the same time, he tells us about some who in the midst of hell managed to laugh, extend themselves, and instead of grabbing more than one share, shared their last piece of bread and watery soup. Viktor Frankl, like so many other successful people before us teaches us that, it is not circumstances and other people's behavior that determines how we feel and act, but how we choose to communicate those circumstances to ourselves.

> *"The quality of your communication determines the quality of your life*
> -TONY ROBBINS

So far, we have learned that our feelings are the result of our internal communication, namely the questions we ask ourselves and the meanings we assign to certain events. If we keep a destructive way of communicating our life, our workplace, or our relationships, it doesn't matter if we go on vacation, take some time off or separate from our partner, as long as our communication remains the same, the same unwanted feelings will return. However, if we learn to develop our self-communication, we like Viktor Frankl will be able to find an empowering meaning even in a place like Auschwitz.

So how can we deal with our unwanted feelings in a way that makes us feel free and satisfied while making other people feel satisfied as well? Here are six common ways in which most of us deal with unwanted feelings. Which way do you seem to be the most fruitful way to handle unwanted feelings?

Avoiding

This is where we try not to feel unwanted feelings. In our attempt not to have feelings such as rejection, disappointment, and frustration, we start avoiding certain people, situations, and contexts, with which we associate unwanted feelings. Avoiding usually leads to giving up trying and believing. The "avoiding" strategy makes life shallow and keeps people from developing intimate relationships or following their passion.

Sharing and Comparing

Some of us like to share and compare with others how bad we feel. We can say things like, "You think your day was bad, wait until you hear about mine." Many of us love to share our unwanted feelings because it makes us feel connected so we don't have to feel bad alone.

Venting

This is when we express everything we feel. We confront people with our feelings. We accuse and hold other people responsible for what we feel. Expressing our feelings as soon as they appear might seem as a good way to get rid of unwanted feelings, but is it really? Have you ever experienced an occasion where you acted on your feelings and said something hurtful, only to find out afterwards that you did not have all the information? And how many of us like being wrong? Instead of being wrong we often start justifying our behavior, and say things like, "Ok, maybe you did not do it this time, but you have done it before." To express our initial feelings might make us feel good for the moment, but if we want to feel good and strengthen our relationships long-term, it is not preferable.

Suppressing

We bury our unwanted feelings and call it "emotional control." But what happens if we continuously stack and suppress our unwanted feelings inside of us? Pressure builds and eventually we run the risk of "exploding." We explode because of something that could have been handled much more effectively at an earlier stage.

Enduring

Instead of finding out the meaning of our feelings, we pretend that "it doesn't feel that bad." We might not complain in the open, but storing it within creates a toxic environment inside of us and soon enough we start thinking about how horrible things are or how horrible people are treating us. This approach usually leads to bitterness.

In the light of all the above, we understand that avoiding, venting, suppressing, and enduring our feelings are not preferable methods if we want to cultivate well-being for us and others long-term.

To Learn

This is when we learn from our feelings. We strive to listen and understand the messages contained by our feelings and utilize the information to better our lives. All of our feelings contain messages. Learning from our feelings is a crucial step if we aspire sustainable wellbeing and emotional freedom.

The secret is to understand and transform the meaning we give our feelings. As long as our feelings have an unwanted meaning, it doesn't matter whether we choose to express them or keep them inside, unwanted feelings will always come back as long as we keep unwanted meanings. Suppressing our feelings, is just a way of maintaining a destructive meaning as we try to ignore how it makes us feel. Transforming feelings is not about "making up" new meanings but rather understanding and learning what our feelings truly means.

HOW DO FEELINGS APPEAR?

The impact of our feelings on our lives makes it essential to understand firstly, how our feelings come to be. Our feelings can be understood as the result of our brain's attempt to interpret and label the information that our senses collect. This is how it works:

1. Every second our senses register millions of external stimuli/pieces of information about the outside world.

2. This information is converted to electrochemical impulses that trigger physiological reactions in our bodies, which make us experience different physical states. These physical states are what we call emotions.

3. It is not until our brain give these emotions a meaning that we experience a feeling. In short, our feelings reflect the label we attach to our physiological states.

This might explain how two people can have the same physical experience but go through two completely different feelings. Different feelings are due to difference in labeling. For example, two people attend a rock concert. For one such concert is a heavenly enjoyable experience, while for the other it is a "highway to hell." The volume of the music might be the same, the blazing spotlight might be the same, and the rocking audiences might be the same, but still, they are experiencing two completely different feelings. One person experiencing freedom, adrenaline, and a sense of community while the other may experience discomfort, fear, and claustrophobia. People's emotional experience is determined by the meaning they label their physiological state.

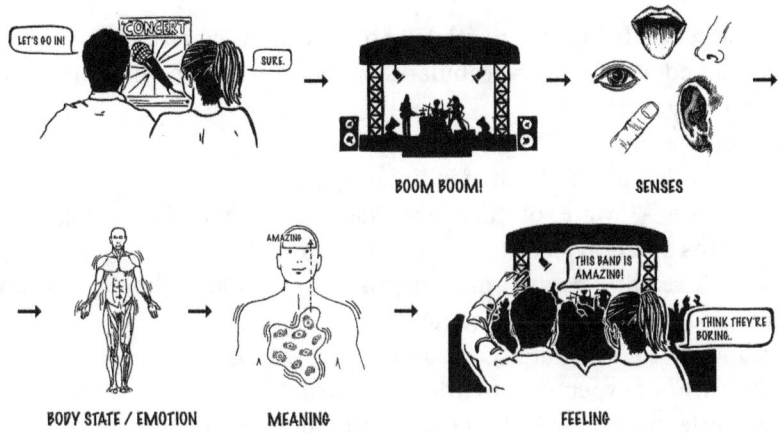

How our feelings appear

Image: Simeon From

Our emotions can be seen as physical activity that can be objectively measured, while our feelings are more subjective since they are the result of our personal way of labeling our emotions. The label we give our emotions becomes our feelings, our feelings become our experience. The good news is, we can become conscious and take full control of our own labeling process.

Most of us are familiar with the term IQ (Intelligence Quotient). IQ could in general terms be defined as a person's ability learn, think abstract, understand causation and to effectively make use of experience.

IQ was long considered by researchers to be the explanatory factor whether a person would become successful or not. That was before emotional intelligence (EQ) became part of the discussion. The concept of EQ became known when scientists were trying to understand how people with medium-high IQ often performed better career-wise than people with high IQ (70% of the time). So what is emotional intelligence?

It is a person's ability to understand, label, regulate, and express his or her emotions. People with high EQ usually share the following characteristics:

1. Empathetic - being able to relate to others and their situation
2. Developed emotional vocabulary, enabling them to pinpoint what they really feel
3. Difficult to offend
4. Open to change and flexible in times of adjustment
5. Self-aware - aware of their weakness and strengths. Using their strengths and don't let their weaknesses stop them
6. Good at reading people - not surprised by people's behavior and understand what motivates people
7. Balanced - know what is good and act accordingly
8. Give without expecting anything in return
9. Not perfectionists, they know perfection does not exist
10. Have understood the power of thought and thus leave no room for negativity
11. Joyous - their joy is rooted in their independent self-worth.

Emotional intelligence is essential in all communications. People with high EQ have a developed ability to control their behavior, manage complex social situations, and make more decisions that lead to desired results in their lives.

The ability to understand the meaning of your feelings will make your feelings an asset instead of an obstacle in the communication with others. The key is to realize that all communication with others starts with the communication with yourself. Once again, the way we communicate the world to ourselves will determine how we feel, how we feel will shape the way we act, which in turn will determine our results, the results we get become our lives. In short, the quality of our communication is directly related to the quality of our life.

YOUR WORDS BECOME YOUR FEELINGS

To master the communication with yourself (your self-communication), is the prerequisite in order to continuously be able to feel wonderful no matter the circumstances. As said earlier, a large part of the way we communicate with ourselves is to label our emotions (physical states). The way we label our emotions is by using words; ***The words you use to describe your*** *emotions, become your feelings.* People who lack words to describe their emotions tend to misunderstand their emotions to a great extent, which increases irrational choices and counter-productive actions.

> "The words you speak creates the world in which you live"
> –MAGGIE WARELL

If you say to yourself, "I am so horribly angry and humiliated," you will most likely experience much anger and humiliation. If instead, you say, "I feel a bit misunderstood," you will have a complete different experience. The words you use to describe your emotions determine what you feel and what you feel determines what you do. In other words, we ought to be careful of the words we are using when describing what we feel to ourselves. Are you incredibly annoyed or incredibly fascinated? The same situation, but different ways to name the emotion and the results in two different emotional experiences, it´s our choice!

According to the Oxford Dictionaries, the English language consists of 170,000 words; a few hundred of which serves to describe our feelings. The average person tends to use only a dozen out of those words to describe his or her emotional experience. An interesting study conducted in US prisons shows that physical violence was one of the most common ways of expressing painful feelings among prison inmates. The survey noted that most feelings related to discomfort, were often channeled through violent acts to a greater extent. In other words, a limited ability to understand, label and express feelings in words made violence the main way to express feelings.

Have you come across someone who always seems to be angry, frustrated, stressed or sad? A common reason to why some people continually experience the same feelings is because they use the same words to describe different emotional experiences. We lump many different experiences together under the same label. The better we can describe and label our feelings the richer emotionally we will be.

NEGATIVE FEELINGS DO NOT EXIST

How can you understand and label your feelings in a more accurate way? All right, now, take out a pen and you can use an empty page in the back of this book. Write at the top of the page "Negative Feelings" under the heading write down five feelings you had during the past week that you consider to be negative. Do it now. Come on! I´ll be waiting for you.

Now that you have written down five "negative" feelings that you had over the last week, I want you to cross over the first part of the heading, namely "Negative" so that it just says, "Feelings." The first step to effectively use our feelings is to understand that there are no negative feelings, *our feelings exist to help us*. A healthy emotional life requires that we understand our feelings and learn how to use them. When we do, we don't have to see our feelings as something negative, but as something that has valuable messages about how we must act in order to feel good.

It is also important to understand that feelings are not a substitute for logic, they are not viruses that we must protect ourselves from, or the product of people's wimsical thinking. Our feelings carry important messages about how we can create a better quality of life. When we begin to understand the messages that our feelings carry, they stop being our enemies but become our allies instead. They become our friends, coaches, and will be able to help us in life's most beautiful and toughest moments. The skill of transforming our feelings will enable us to live a life where the circumstances do not shape us, but where we shape the circumstances.

All "negative" and unwanted feelings are messages from our brain to do one of the following:

- Change the way we see the situation
- Change the way we act in the situation

Just as we understand our body by studying the structure of our muscles (anatomy), we can understand our feelings by studying, "The Anatomy of our Feelings," namely what our feelings are made of.

When was the last time you had a painful feeling? Was it after a quarrel, when someone did not understand you or when you experienced time pressure? The source of most of our painful feelings is basically the feeling of being hurt in some way and we can only feel hurt if we feel like we have lost something. In short, our painful feelings are rooted in the feeling of loss. We may feel that we lost time, love, hope, joy, our value, confidence, trust, belief in ourselves or people's respect. Sometimes we manage to feel loss over things we never even had in the first place, "I lost my chance," "my opportunity" or "my goal." Have you experienced that? Maybe it was a summer day and you had imagined perfect weather and a nice day at the beach, but instead, the rain came pouring down. Suddenly you get the feeling that you lost a day at the beach. But can we really lose something that we never had? Of course not. To experience loss, we need to communicate to ourselves that we have lost something.

Have you heard anybody say, "I lost love", "she took my happiness" or "they took my dignity?" Isn't it interesting how we can think that people can take something that is created on the inside of us? The only reason why we feel loss is because we have given it the meaning of loss. Many of us, however, have become experts in creating the illusion of loss.

Even our the "Laws of Physics" make it quite clear that nothing can be lost (The Law of Conservation of Mass). Nothing in the entire universe ever disappears. It can be transformed but never disappear. Just like water becomes steam, our feelings can be transformed, the good news is, we get to decide into what.

Therefore, many of the painful feelings we experience on a daily basis are caused by our own ideas about how people and life should be? We develop rules about how life, the weather, and people should be in order for us to be happy, and whenever they don't meet our expectations, we give ourselves the reason to feel sad, angry or disappointed. For example, when a loved one passes away.

For example when a relative passes away. This is usually a moment in time where many of us experience a tangible sense of loss. But, shouldn't it be the other way around. That every minute we had to spend with that person was a minute won. Painful feelings tell us less about the outside world and more about the rules and expectations we have on the outside world.

> *The only thing we can really lose is*
> *our expectations on how things should be.*
> – NOAH FROM

The problem is not our rules or expectations in itself, but rather, that we base them on how we think things should be, instead of understanding how things really work. To base our emotional wellbeing on how we think it should be, would be equally intelligent as a farmer who sows a seed one day and the next day comes back and goes into a fit because the soil hasn't produced any fruit over night. The key to sustainable wellbeing lies in the understanding of how things really work and then operate in alignment with that.

After all, the entire universe is governed by basic laws. The laws of gravitation, electricity and about velocity. In light of this, we understand that everything in our lives are limited by these laws of nature. These laws are what the philanthropist Jim Rohn calls "The Set Up." Our emotional wellbeing say less about the world and more about our understanding and to what extent we act in accordance with the setup of the world. We don´t have to like "The Set Up" but the best advice we can adopt is "Don´t try to fool it," it won´t work. The farmer doesn´t need to like the law of sowing and reaping, but if he wants to harvest, he needs to learn how it works and the act accordingly.

"THE FEEL-TRANSFORMER" -HOW TO DEAL WITH UNWANTED FEELINGS

So how do we deal with feelings like sadness, depression or stress and transform them into something that can help us? First of all, it is good to know that we always have the right to be sad, depressed, and worried. These emotions are a big and important part of the human experience. However, the chances are extremely low that such feelings will help us to live a wonderful life if we remain in them.

Successful people before us have shown how we can transform our "negative" emotions into fuel on our journey towards a emotional wellbeing. We will call this method, "The Feel-Transformer" (created by Tony Robbins and modified by me). The Feel-Transformer consists of six steps that if we start applying today, we extract the precious information that our feelings carry. The more times we use it, the easier and more natural it will become. Take your time and start transforming your feelings today!*

Select an undesirable feeling that you've been wrestling with lately. To transform the feeling into a helpful message just follow the steps below:

1. ***Identify the True Feeling***- Here is where you find out what you really feel. When you experience an unwanted feeling, you always start by asking yourself the question: "What do I really feel?" You have already established that all "negative" feelings originate from the feeling of hurt, which in turn is rooted in the feeling of loss. No matter what unwanted feeling you experience, it is rooted in the feeling of loss of something.

---

* T. Robbins, Awaken The Giant Within, p. 251, New York: Summit Books 1991.

2. ***Appreciate the Feeling*** - When you receive an unwanted feeling, you need not suppress it, share it, ignore it, or feel bad because you feel as we do. Since you now know that your feelings are there to help you, it becomes natural to be grateful for the valuable message that feelings have for you. You can be thankful, because it is a message about how you can improve your life.

3. ***Get Incredibly Curious*** - As children, we were all like little detectives. We wanted to know everything. Now is the time to become as children again, get curious. Curiosity makes you more open to new knowledge. Start by asking the question: "What is the actual message this feeling is trying to give me? What is it I feel that I have lost? Certainty? Possibility? Other people's affirmation? Am I afraid of losing something in the future?" When you have identified the reason for the sense of loss you have, you can choose to remain in the feeling and let it torture you or read the message it has for you about how you can get rid of it. Remember, your "negative" feelings are instructions to do one of two things: A) Change your perception of the situation, or (B) Change your approach and way of acting.

4. ***Become Certain That You Can Handle This Feeling*** - Now that you know what the message your feeling wants to give you, the next step is to be sure that you can deal with this feeling. This you can do by remembering a time in the past when you successfully managed to deal with this feeling in a good way. Many of us are often very good at remembering all the times we felt bad and are afraid to end up there again, but it is key that you remember the occasions when you have been able to manage your feelings in a fruitful manner and use those as resources to cope with the situations you find yourself in. Close your eyes if necessary and remember a situation where you had this feeling and were able to handle it in a way that made you feel good. What did you do? What needed to happen? Did you change the way you imagine the situation or did you change your way of acting? When we see how we have resolved a similar situation in the past, we train our brain to associate the unwanted feeling with a solution.

5. ***Get Absolutely Certain That You Can Handle This feeling In The Future*** - Now, it is time to practice at solving a similar situation in the future. Our brain doesn't know the difference between reality and what it vividly imagines. If you allow your brain to rehearse how to handle simi-

lar situations in the future, your brain will easily be able to deal with such a situation whenever they happen in the future. Knowing how to handle the situation in the future will allow you to be certain even in uncertain situations. Now, select a new situation that in the future could make you feel this way and see yourself handling the situation in a way that makes you feel good while achieving a desired result. Now when you see yourself succeed, ask yourself, "How did I have to perceive the situation? What did I have to do?" You have now created a future strategy on how to handle this feeling in the future.

6. **Design a Beautiful Life**- Now when you have extracted the valuable information from your feeling and know how to act, there is only one thing remaining. Action. Decide to act on this information and you will experience miracles.

The following steps will work for any "negative" emotion you have. The perfect strategy to get depressed is not to follow these steps, but remain in the swamp of unwanted feelings. If we keep our perception and continue to act as we have always done, we will automatically experience the same feelings and hinder ourselves from living a wonderful life. It's when we remain in our "negative" feelings that we start to believe that there is nothing we can do and no way out of feeling bad. By transforming our feelings messages, we are able to always find our way back to a place where we feel good no matter the circumstances.

"The Feel Transformer" is the method that terminates misunderstandings, destructive meanings, and allows us to transform our feelings instead of suppressing them, so that they can help us to handle situations better. In the beginning it might feel a bit time consuming, but believe me, it will soon become a way of thinking. The Feel Transformer is a tool for those who wish to increase their EQ. How many times a day do we end up in situations where we experience feelings we don't really want? We get annoyed in traffic, at the coffee break, at our colleagues, and at the airport. Now, we can, if we choose it, learn to deal with those feelings and turn them into instructions on how to act in order to feel like we want.

The Feel-Transformer can be summed up by the following:

1. Identify the feeling- What is it that you really feel?
2. Appreciate the feeling - All your feelings exist to help and tell you something.

3. Get curious-Find out what the emotional message really mean.
4. Get certain that you can handle the feeling - Learn from how you've dealt with this feeling in the past. Model it.
5. Get absolutely certain that you can handle this feeling in the future - Imagine and repeat solving situations like these in the future.
6. Design your life – Take action on the information that you have extracted. and improve your life.

If we change the meaning of the event, all of our experiences of the event will change. Remember, nothing has a meaning in itself, but everything gets the meaning that we give it! When we become emotionally intelligent, we understand that the meanings we give initially are not the absolute truth. People with high EQ has therefore developed the ability that in difficult situations find an alternative meaning by asking themselves the question: What else could this mean? This helps our brain to remember that our initial meaning is not absolutely true. When people behave badly, it does not mean that they want to hurt us. People are not their behaviors. Haven't you ever behaved badly, for no reason, but maybe because you were stressed, tired or hungry? We all have. Things don't always mean what we think they mean, so we better choose meanings that make us feel good while we figure out what things really mean.

Good external communication assumes good internal communications. The better we understand what is going on inside, the better we can communicate with the outside. The more we develop our emotional labeling, the better we become at communicating our feelings without feeling hurt or hurting others. This will result in a bigger sense of freedom in our communication, in a way that few people have experienced.

So next time, before we react for King and country, we can through a simple question find out the true meaning of our feelings. As soon as we experience something that triggers feelings such as anger, sadness or disappointment, let it be an alarm clock to ask yourself the question: What else could this mean? And to find out, we can use "The Feel-Transformer."

For example, if you and your partner have reserved a table at a romantic restaurant. You have already arrived, time passed, and your partner didn't show. Suddenly you feel how it begins to bubble within you and soon enough, you feel angry with your partner for not being on time. When your partner later arrived after 30 minutes, you have built up so much frustration that you snap and start eating in silence. Why does this happen? Because of the meaning you have given your partner's late arrival, of course. Maybe you have managed to give your partner's late arrival the meaning that he does not care about your agreement or even that he does not take you seriously. Remember, unwanted feelings are rooted in our feeling hurt because we feel that we have lost something.

Instead of getting caught up in a vicious spiral of negative feelings, we can now initiate a Feel-Transformation by asking the question: What else can this mean? In this way, we can remind ourselves that all "negative feelings" are basically messages that ask us to alter either our perception of the situation or our current actions. But changing the way one thinks and the meaning is not always easy to do. So what do we do when we can't do something ourselves? We ask each other for help.

The best sign of maturity is responsibility. Our goal is to take responsibility for what we feel while we receive help to understand the actual facts. Decision based on actual facts is the best ground in which fruitful communication can grow. Since we don't always know 100 percent the reason behind our partner's behavior, we do best in assigning an empowering meaning meanwhile finding out the facts. People tend to be whatever we make them. Our status quo should not be suspicion but rather expect that our partner has acted with good intention. When we feel good, we can act more fruitful. It could look like this: Your partner arrives late to the restaurant, you would like to sit down and when the opportunity arises, so say:

> "Honey, I need your help. Somehow I was able to interpret your late arrival as if you didn´t care. I know that is not true because I know you think I'm valuable. But I need your help, would you like to help me understand what happened?"

Over explicit? Maybe, but very effective. Through this way of communication we remind ourselves of the truth, it is in fact, we, who are responsible for how we feel. This is a way to communicate where we can express our feelings in a way that makes us feel good, that creates proximity, connection, and get our partners to feel important. We also get a more authentic picture of the situation, which creates better grounds on which we can decide on how to act. When we stop reacting to the environment and start taking responsibility for what we feel, the wiser decisions we will make. As we get better at understanding our feelings, they cease to be an obstacle for us, in our relationships, in our workplace, and in our lives, and instead become instructions on how we can improve the quality of our lives.

But do we always have to question other people's behavior? Not at all, if we become good at transforming our feelings and assigning empowering meanings, there will be no reason to question people's behavior. Our partner's late arrival can, of course, mean that "they don't care," but it can also mean that the situation will be an opportunity to deepen our relationship or "they are doing their best to be here." The power to transform our feelings lies in our hands.

Have you ever forgot why you are communicating while you are communicating? Communication comes from the Latin word, "communicare" which means, "to make common." The goal of communication between people is to get a common view and understanding of the situation. A clear common image assumes that we individually have a clear inner image. That being said, the first step of effective external communication begins with effective internal communication.

Successful communication between people is all about building bridges. People's different backgrounds and agendas make it important to build bridges between each other's context. It's like if we all come from different worlds, we then must therefore, build bridges between us and the other person's world. Communication is not about convincing one another that our world is true, but rather asking for more information about their world while clarifying our world. In this way, we can understand and relate to each other in a better way on the journey to design a wonderful life no matter the circumstances.

TAKE AWAYS

Just as fever and headaches are symptoms of an underlying cause, our feelings are symptoms of an underlying cause. Our feelings are symptoms of our own way of communicating events to ourselves. We communicate to ourselves by giving events different meanings. Nothing has any meaning except the meaning we give it. The meanings we give situations, people, and happenings determine how we feel about them.

Feelings exist to help us, "Negative" feelings are nothing more than messages about what we need to do to feel good again. If we don't learn to use the practical messages that our feelings carry, we will soon start to think that our feelings are beyond our control.

"The Feel Transformer" is an effective tool that helps us to understand our feelings and transform them into practical messages that we can use to understand what to do. A wonderful life starts with knowing what you really feel, why, and how you can change that.

We are the source of everything we feel, and therefore we have the ability to create all the feelings we want, whenever we want and wherever we want.

CHAPTER 4

A WINNING STATE

THE KEY TO YOUR INNER RESOURCES

By assigning situations empowering meanings, we can change the way we feel in a heartbeat. At the same time, we all know that life will bring us situations where it seems almost impossible to give empowering meanings, what do we do then?

During my youth, I worked at the movie theatre in Malmö, Sweden. It was a place where people would come to dream away for a while, take a trip to a magical place and escape reality for a moment. My passion for storytelling took me from being responsible for the popcorn to spend most of my time presenting and introducing the films for the cinema audience.

Every day was packed with new and exciting premieres, everything from laugh-friendly love comedies, heartbreaking drama, action-packed thrillers to adventure movies. The films were many and varied, just like the audience. Some movies attracted an older audience who quietly ate their popcorn while they enjoyed the last independent movie. Other films attracted testosterone pumped, fizzy drinking, and gun loving action fans, who wanted guns, muscles, and fights to the death. In all of this, I took on a mission, to always, regardless the audience, give them a "once in a lifetime" film presentation.

I still remember my first cinema presentation. I felt good and ready. Unsuspected, my first presentation was in front of a "testosterone" audience. With our biggest cinema hall packed, chips bags rustling, and the sodas flowing, I entered the stage and stepped in front of the cinema screen, and the headlights went on. "Ladies and gentlemen, welcome to the best cinema in Malmö! Tonight we will be cast into an adventure of life and death …" The rest of the presentation did not turn out quite as I'd imagined. The little feeling of uncertainty that I had felt before the presentation took over and turned a well prepared and brilliant presentation into a white, skinny guy's attempt to be funny. In short, the "testosterones" were not impressed. The receipt of their discontent was a symphony of booing and a rain of popcorn, sweets, and candies. It was like in a movie and the nerd, the new enthusiastic presenter had to escape the cinema hall under fire.

The week after the action movies seemed to be in the minority and I enjoyed making the pensioners giggle and feel comfortable. However, the city and billboards were covered in advertising an upcoming film that made me realize that I would soon be facing my biggest challenge so far. The film was called "Immortals." The movie was the story about a young man selected by the Greek god Zeus to defeat the bloodthirsty and power-hungry King Hyperion and his endless army. While the commercials promised a movie full of muscles, sweat, and heroism, I knew that I was facing another war against a bloodthirsty cinema audience.

Saturday would come, and it was time for the premiere. I was ready and prepared for anything that might happen. This audience in Malmö was infamous. My colleagues gathered up and were just as excited as I was. When advertising and the previews had ended, and the curtain closed, it was time. Suddenly, I realized, *if it's war I am going into, I have to become a warrior*. Quickly, I pulled off my neat, butler looking cinema vest and tore off my stylish shirt and asked my colleague Felix to fetch me the lid of a trash bin, while I equipped myself with a spear, which really was mop. I made some explosive push-ups while I heard the crowd started to get impatient. I felt more ready than ever. I flung up the doors and rushed down and took the stage armed with my trash bin lid and my mop. "Ladies and gentlemen, my name is Noaidis and I'm the theatre's best warrior," I commanded confidently. "Tonight everybody will throw their rubbish in the recycle bins and exit by using the rearmost end." The crowd was in shock over the pale, pumped-up presenter who, like a lion was moving across the stage. A murmur started to spread among the seats while I continued. "Tonight all of us are part of one single army. Tonight, we are all warriors. TONIGHT, WE ARE IMMORTALS!!!" What followed gave me goose bumps across my entire body. I was witnessing a full theater of 350 people who stood up and roared as if they were facing life's last battle and during their exultation and ROAR I stormed out with fixed step out of the salon.

THE DIFFERENCE IN PEOPLE´S LIVES

What is the difference between situations where we feel like we are making a fool of ourselves and situations where we just feel like we are delivering at our full capacity? How can it be, we are the same person with the same capacity and internal resources, but still…? *The difference is the state we are in.*

Can you recall a time when it felt like everything went wrong? An event where you blacked out? It might have been a business meeting, a tennis match or a situation where you felt completely lost? A situation in which you afterwards might have asked yourself, "Why did I say or do that?" In contrast to this, most of us can remember a time when everything just went great and it felt like we were in "flow." Maybe it was a time when we practiced a sport or delivered on a presentation or in a meeting. We saw things that nobody else saw, came up with solutions that no one thought of and felt like the Sheriff of town. What was the difference? The difference was the State we were in.

Our State (short for neuro-physiological state) is the sum of all ongoing neurophysiological processes in our body, namely the sum of all the sensations and nerve signals going on at the same time. All of our feelings such as passion, love, happiness, casual, power, respect, and sadness are really just different states.

Stop for a minute ask yourself: "Could it be that in everything I do, I am limited by the state I am in?

Try this thought: In everything we do, we are driven by changing our state.

Our entire life is a pursuit for different states. If you think about it, our life consist of different, learned behaviors on how to achieve a desired state. When we feel hungry, unproductive, lazy, tired, sad, angry, bored or any other unwanted condition, we all have our own way of changing that state.

There are endless ways to change our state. People throughout history have been willing to try everything in order to get into a desired state; sex, sports, meditation, drugs, bungee jumping, and more. An important note to make is: that much of what we use in order to change our state have limitations they are often quick fixes, short term solutions, and based on external factors.

Ask yourself, "What do I do to get me into a more desired state? Watch series, read, exercise, sleep, eat, dance, smoke, fight, work, drink or indulge in coffee?"

Talking about states, we can understand that there are no angry, depressed or selfish people, there are just angry, depressed and selfish states. We all commute between different states and different states make us behave in different ways. A depressed person can rage out in anger and even laugh once in a while. A person who smokes, do not smoke all the time, but smoke only when he or she is in a state of wanting to smoke. Its the same way with a person that over eats, the person does not eat every single minute, but only when he or she is in a state where they feel like eating. Other times they are in another state and do other things.

Most of us slip unconsciously in and out of states. Sometimes we feel good, and sometimes we feel bad without realizing that our state is a power that we can learn to use. Becoming aware, taking charge and learning to use our states enables us to utilize the resources we have on the inside whenever we need.

What is the cost of not controlling our own state? What does Jimmy Hendrix, Marilyn Monroe, Janis Joplin, John Belushi, Elvis Presley, Heath Ledger, Robin Williams, Avicci (Tim Berling) have in common? They are all people who never learned how to manage their state. They are people who had all the reason in the world to be happy (by everybody else's standard), but lived in states, which in the end made them kill themselves. They got to be creative, met new people, they had money, families, and people that loved them, but in the end that wasn't enough. They all tried to use external things to solve an internal unrest.

> "The quality of our lives reflects the quality of the states
> we experience in on a daily basis."
> –TONY ROBBINS

Our states shapes our entire lives. Someone once said, "Our lives are the sum of all experienced states." Our states become the limitation or the key to our inner resources. Our states determine our behavior, our behavior determine our results and the results constitutes our lives.

A wonderful life consists of wonderful states and wonderful states are no coincidence. A sustainable wonderful life begins with the awareness of the states we find ourselves in on a daily basis. It starts with a simple question: What state am I in right now? A stressed state? A state of fear? An angry state? An invincible state? A wonderful state?

MASTER YOUR LIFE EXPERIENCE

So, if our state is the key to our inner capacity, wouldn't it be great if we knew how to get ourselves into a wonderful and motivated state whenever we wanted to, regardless of resources or circumstances? The good news is that we can. The first step to master our own state is to understand and learn how to master its key components:

- Your Internal Representations =WHAT and HOW your *re-presentor imagine* situations in your head.

- Your physiology= How you move, how you make use of your body, breathing and face.

Our Internal Representations
Not long ago, there was a terrorist attack in Stockholm, Sweden. It constitutes a practical example of state change. The situation was uncertain and shocking for everybody, but people's state varied massively. Some would get into a state of anxiety and worry, others into a state of anger and rage, while others into a state of compassion and courage. People's state depended on what and how they imagined the situation. How they *re-presented* the situation to themselves.

An individual´s internal representations become her reality. Fear limits more people than anything else. But fear is nowhere near as complicated as we make it. Fear is most times us imagining something that hasn't happened in a way that frightens us. In other words, fear is just the result of our internal representations.

The impact of our internal representation can be exemplified by the following: When our partner comes home late from work, it is our internal representation that will determine how we treat them. How do you think we would treat them if we had an internal representation of he or she having an affair with someone else? Would we act differently if we instead imagined our partner doing everything he or she could to get home and care for us? The difference in our behavior is always rooted in the internal representation we are using.

But what determines how we imagine things then? Our internal representations are much characterized by our upbringing and our environment. For example, when you were little, if your mom sometimes came home late and your dad reacted by saying, "She is probably shopping and thinking about herself," it is very likely that you learned that when people come home late, they do it because they are selfish. Whereas if your father always responded by saying "Oh mom is working late again, she is a true hero working so hard so we can live well," your imagination of "latecomers" will probably be different.

A person who experience depression often uses internal representations, which result in misery. Depressed people are experts in creating internal representations of lack of control and resources. They vividly imagine themselves as unable to cope with the present and all the future shoulds and musts. How would you feel if you pictured yourself unable to cope with anything? Pretty depressed, right?

Stress and depression are not absolute states which cannot be changed. All of our painful feelings are really just messages asking us to review our internal representation. Depression for example, can be viewed as a message telling us that it is not healthy to imagine life as one big chunk to be solved all at once. The first step out of a depression always begins with a manageable and hopeful representation of the future. When the person experiencing the depression succeeds in prioritizing and complete the first little thing on the list the person will feel better.

Physiology
Something, which affects our state to an even greater extent, is how we use our physiology, namely, what we do with our bodies, our posture, muscles, tone of voice, how we breathe, move, drink, and eat. Let me give an example.

If I asked you to describe a depressed person who stood hiding behind a curtain, I am pretty sure that you could make a pretty accurate description. Does the person usually have a proud or weak posture? Head up or down? Breathing full or shallow? Does the person speak loud and clear or low and vague?

See, a person's emotional life is often limited to how the person uses his or her physiology throughout the day. A person who experience depression has to use their body in a "depressed" way. A person with limited movement patterns will have a limited emotional life, hence the cliché but nevertheless true "motion drives emotion."

Our mind and body are in constant interaction. Our internal representations will influence our physiology, and our physiology will affect our internal representations. An evident example of this is when we are sick. Can you remember the last time you were sick or nauseous? Did you feel like cracking new award winning ideas or travelling around the world? Most likely not, you just wanted to get well. When we experience muscular tension, fatigue or illness, we tend to magnify negative internal representations, which in turn affects our states. The states we experience determine how we act and our actions determine our results.

Researchers Amy J. C. Cuddy, Caroline A. Wilmuth and Dana R. Carney of Harvard University did a study in how our physiology in the form of "power poses" (different body postures) affects our behavior and consequently our professional results. (You may have seen Amy Cuddy´s TED talk). The study shows that a radical change in a person's physiology and a more open posture produces feelings of dominance and help us dare to take greater risks, we become more action-oriented, enjoy increased pain tolerance and increase in testosterone.

Image: Roberto Schmidt, AFP, Getty Images

Image: Xinhua

Athletes constantly put themselves into powerful states through the way they use their bodies.

A radical change in our physiology makes us not just to feel more powerful but produce actual hormones and substance in our body that makes us stronger and energetic. In contrast, a closed posture to testosterone, our dominance hormone is dropping markedly and instead, we produce cortisol, a stress hormone that becomes fuel for feelings such as anxiety and stress. Cortisol also suppresses your immune system. Successful leaders have learned the importance of owning their state. The way we use our body effects our entire biochemistry and therefore also the way we feel physically.*

When we understand the physiological impact on our mental health and our emotional life, we understand the importance of taking care of our body. Many people think that exercising is about six pack, broad shoulders, and a nice bum, but tend to forget that a good physique is a prerequisite for a healthy emotional life and mental well-being.

DECIDE TO LIVE A WONDERFUL LIFE

My grandfather always used to say, "A healthy body is a highway to happiness and dirt road to stress." The challenge we face today is that a growing number of people are creating a dirt road to happiness and a highway to stress by the way we use our body. My grandfather's words carry an important lesson. Creating healthy routines, doing a little exercise every day, and eating healthily, will create the foundation for emotional well-being.

We don't have to be people who wake up in the morning, keep our fingers crossed and hoping for a good day. Such an attitude makes us a victim of circumstances. It becomes a life in reaction where we feel according to our enviroment and where circumstances determine the quality of our lives. In light of this, ask yourself the question: What will it cost me emotionally, mentally, socially and physically if I do not learn how to master my own state? What will it cost my parter? My children?

Now, imagine the reward if we started to learn how to master our own state, if we learned how to get into a beautiful state no matter where we are. A statewhere we feel confident, strong, loved, and motivated. Are you willing to do it?

*J. C. Cuddy, A. Wilmuth & R. Carney, Harvard Business School Working Paper, No. 13-027, September 2012.

To live life in a beautiful state starts with us deciding to do so, no matter what. Next step in order to master our state, is to learn to master our imaginations and our physiology. In order to learn to control our imaginations, we must first understand what we use to imagine.

Like most animals, we as human beings use our senses to register and interpret our surroundings. Without our senses, our nervous system would never get any information. Every second, our brain sifts among millions collected data ranging from the blood flowing through our fingers to the birds singing outside the window. Each second our conscious mind handles approximately 40 bits of information per second while our unconscious processes 11 million pieces of information per second. Our brain filters information based on what it needs or think it needs in the future. Our brain generalizes, modifies, and distorts all the information and then creates internal representations. The way we represent reality to ourselves reflects very seldom the reality as such but rather, it reflects our personal interpretation of reality. *In short, our image of reality is rarely the reality in actuality, but only one of millions of possible interpretations of reality.*

Since we almost never know how things really are, wouldn't it be better to imagine them in a way that empowers us? When we learn to master our internal representations and our physiology, we will be able to get into a state and maximize our resources as human beings regardless of circumstances. When successful people face difficult or challenging situations, they could of course, choose to imagine the situation in a way that makes them doubtful, frustrated, or even want to give up, but they don't. Instead, they create internal representations of how they make it through, which produces optimistic state and fuels them to act constructively.

Our brain doesn't know the difference between reality and what we vividly imagine. When a horrible situation takes place, it is therefore, the ability to master our perception and physiology that will determine how we feel.

> *"As a man thinketh in his heart, so is he"*
> – PROVERBS 23:7

I am sure you have heard people explain their behavior by saying, "It's just the way I am". That is not true at all. Not a single human being is a rigid unchangable object. Who we are is not a coincidence. Neuroscientists shows us that our thoughts and the way we represent life reinforces and creates new neural pathways in our brain. These neural pathways determine which states that will become less or more available to us and therefore will to a large extent determine how you act. This means, that we are the result of our thoughts and the way we represent life to ourselves.

We always perform in accordance with the signals we send to the brain; the good news is that this is a process that we can take control of and develop. By consciously creating internal representations that strengthen us (even in difficult situations) we challenge our nervous system to use specific nerve pathways continuously. By doing this daily, we will create a major neurological highways to beautiful states. Suddenly, empowering states can become a natural part of our lives, something we can come back to even in times of grief, exhaustion, and despair if we wish to.

If we want to, we can live in wonderful states no matter the circumstances since we have the capacity to create the sensory input we want by consciously training our internal representation and the way we use our body. The more often we find ourselves in beautiful states, the more beautiful life gets.

Now, stop and think for a second about the following: Could it be that the quality of the states I'm in on a daily basis determines the quality of my life?

It is true to a large extent. Another important factor is how we choose to channel our states. Once we are in a specific state, our brain makes use of different behavioral options in order to channel different states. Shortly put, our different states are channeled through different behaviors.

Ever since we were kids, we've learned different behaviors through which we channel our states. Some have learned to channel a state of irritation through a violent and aggressive behavior while others become silent and indifferent. Some choose to work out when they become stressed, and others eat, some seek fellowship when feeling alone, others take to the bottle. Our different ways to channel what we feel comes from the behavioral alternatives that we have gathered throughout our lives.

The way you channel your states is limited to the behaviors you have been introduced to. This is why it is so important to take inventory of the friends we spend our time with. Everyone we spend time with introduces new behaviors, through which our states will be expressed. Throughout our upbringing, we absorbed behavior alternatives from our parents, friends, and surroundings.

State mastery becomes possible when we on a daily basis start building neurological highways to fruitful and productive states by:

1. On a daily basis condition our body through a radical change in our physiology. You can change your state and thus your behavior in an instant through movement, breathing, physical exercise or in any way create tension in your body. Next time you experience an unwanted feeling, jump, do some breathing exercises, work out, use your voice, sing or talk loudly. In order to be depressed, we have to move like depressed people do. If we want to be happy, we have to move happily, sing out loud, shout, use our face happily and use your body, do something to get you blood pumping and give your cells life, "Where the body goes, the head will follow." Some think that this sounds ridiculous, and it may be, but it works. Plus, doesn't it sound more ridiculous to feel bad and believe that you can't do anything about it?

2. Regarding our internal representation, we have to on a daily basis train and teach our brains to Re-Present (represent) life in an empowering way. Whether it is Mandela who spent 27 years in prison, Elise who was sexually abused since the age of five or Viktor Frankl who stared death in the face in Auschwitz, they are all people who regardless of circumstances managed to imagine their lives in empowering way. One way of doing this is by taking at least ten minutes a day and:

    A. Find a comfortable yet active sitting position. Hands on your heart and start breathing deeply. While feeling your heart beating, start breathing through your heart. Take time to remember one thing that you could be grateful for. It could be your heart for example. Your heart is a gift, which you've been given without deserving it. It pumps life into your body. It beats 100.000 times a day without you having to think about it. Give thanks for it.

    B. As you continue to breathe through your heart, picture something else that you could be truly grateful for. It can be a memory or a person who you appreciate. It can be the air you are breathing a person in your life or an opportunity. Gratefulness has no limits.

    C. Continue to breathe deeply. When you find something you feel grateful for, imagine it. See it, hear the sound of it, and feel what it feels like, take it all in. Drive the feeling of gratitude deeper into your body. Make it real. New neural pathways are created which makes fruitful states more accessible.

A sailor corrects his course continuously to ensure that the ship reaches port. In the same way, we can ask ourselves, "Am I in a beautiful state right now?" If yes, wonderful, if no GET IN STATE. Create a state of absolute satisfaction by creating radical change in your body and imagine what you love, what you are grateful for, and what you are truly proud of. Move, speak it out loud and picture it vividly.

We have the choice to either let our state be hijacked by everything that is happening around us, or we can take charge of our own state by creating empowering stimuli ourselves.

TAKE AWAYS

The difference between situations where we feel uncertain or "failed" compared to situations where we feel great and deliver at our best is the state we are in. We act in accordance with the state we are in. Our state determines our behavior, our behavior determines our results, and our results constitute our lives. The quality of our states can therefore be seen as determining the quality of our lives.

The good news is that we have the ability to change our state instantly. Through a radical change in our physiology and by creating new internal representations of any situation, we can control our states. This is an ability that we have whether we want it or not. We have access to all the feelings we want to feel and need never be a victim of outside circumstances.
It is not what happens that determines the quality of our life, but how we handle the happening. How well we handle the happening is determined by the state we are in.

Chapter 5

THE ROOT OF ALL GOOD

OUR INNERMOST LONGING

The train rushed through the snow-covered landscape. On the way home from Northern Sweden, I worked on my laptop. While writing, I could not help but notice a man sitting on the other side of the aisle of the train carriage. Sloped down, deeply sighing, staring out into thin air, it was apparent that something was not right. Since I was writing about feelings and state change, I considered it appropriate to ask how the man was doing.

I sat down next to him and fifteen minutes later, I had heard a story about a nasty family drama. The man called himself Danno and came from Kosovo. After telling his family that he was gay, his father had tried to murder him. Danno's mother saved his life, and he managed to escape to Sweden. Danno had now received a penalty notice which forced him to leave Sweden and return to Kosovo, to a country in which his father had sworn to kill him if he got a hold of him.

Evidently and understandably, Danno imagined his life situation in a way that put him in a state of anxiety and suffering and also used his physiology in a way that reinforced that state. His story might justify his condition, but at the same time, I knew that no matter what he was facing, he would need all the inner resources available. He needed to change his state.

I grabbed his arm a little harder than one usually grabs a stranger on the train and looked deep into his eyes and asked, "What are you really grateful for at this moment Danno?" Both Danno and other passengers looked surprised at me. I agree that it may not be the question you expect, after just having described how your whole life is turned upside down, but I knew that changing his state was crucial. If Danno would remain in a state of anxiety and stress, he would deal with the situation in an anxious and stressful way.

I kept my gaze, held his arm, and asked again, "What could you be really grateful for right now?" His voice trembled as he replied, "My boyfriend Tommy" "What about Tommy makes you grateful?" I asked confidently. Danno began to tell the story of a love that was the best thing he knew. A love that was kind and strong. In just a few seconds, his wrinkled, worried face straightened out, his eyes got back the spark, and I saw how he envisioned Tommy.

I wished that I could say that my hour conversation with Danno helped him find the power within himself. The power that enabled him to deal with his situation in a better way. I don't know what happened to Danno. The only thing I know is that my encounter with Danno, holds one of life's most important lesson. All aspired states are accessible within us. The love Danno experiences in relation with Tommy, the heat it spread in his body, the strength it brought to his mind, the peace it brought to his soul it existed within him all along.

Even though most of us may not be under the threat of murder, the story of Danno is a reminder that hard times will happen to us all. Regardless of who we are and where we come from, we will all experience times when our lives are shaken, and everything we rely upon is turned upside down. People in our surrounding can fall ill, the economy might crash, or we might lose our job. Approaching the end of the book, we have learned that we will not always be able to control the events of our lives but we can always decide how to respond to the events. And it is our respons that will determine the quality of our lives. Our ability to handle the events of our lives is determined by the state we are in.

All our states can be divided into the following categories:

- Beautiful states
- States of pain
- States of suffering

Beautiful states are often states of joy, passion, gratitude, peace of mind, and faith. Beautiful states allow us to be the best version of ourselves. They occur when we use our body and mind in an empowering way. Consciously focus on what we want to see more of in our lives and develop the ability to give meanings that strengthen us no matter the circumstances.

States of pain occur when the circumstances do not match how we think life "should" be. State of pain is inevitable, but they don't have to define how we feel. The quality of people's lives is different depending on what they choose to do with their pain. We are at choice, either we let pain result in sadness, disappointment and anger or compassion, awareness, and love.

State of suffering occurs when we stay in our pain, when our circumstances do not match our image of how life "should" be, meanwhile we doubt that it ever will change for the better. Danno was undeniably in a state of suffering.

WHAT IS KEEPING US FROM EXPERIENCING A WONDERFUL LIFE

If beautiful states allow us to maximize our internal resources, what is keeping us from experiencing those states? What is stopping us from being the best we can and courageously live our deepest passion? The answer is fear, namely two fears:

- To not be enough
- To not be loved

The fear of not being enough controls many peoples lives. The fear of not being successful enough, smart enough or good looking enough etc. The fear of not being enough make us spend most of our lives pursuing outer success, to make sure that people perceive us as valuable and irreplaceable.

We want people to accept us and are ready to break our backs to possess qualities people recognize. We want to save the world, build careers, hold a prestigious title, be good parents, become rich, famous, and be seen as smart and sexy. Our quest to feel valuable in the eyes of others often comes at the expense of our own health and not seldom other's well-being.

> *"We want to be loved, in lack of that admired, in lack of that feared, in lack of that hated and despised. We want to instill people some kind of feeling. The soul shudders from the void and want connection whatever the price."*
>
> - HJALMAR SÖDERBERG

Just as the quote implies, our fear of not being loved is so strong that we will do anything to avoid it. Because love can't be bought or demanded but only given, we all feel certain vulnerability in relation to it. When we experience loss of control. In order to gain control again, we tend to choose society's established way to merit love, namely by performance.

Most of us strive to achieve something that we think will make us worthy of love. We may not see our work as a quest to be loved, on the other hand, it is clear that our value in society today is strongly tied to what we are doing or performing. We are judged on the basis of our results, merits, achievements, successes, and titles. In light of this, many of us live in the reality of, "if only I can perform well enough I will be accepted and ultimately worthy of love."

Measuring our value using external factors will make our experience of love limited to the availability of external factors and our ability to perform and attain them. In our fear of not living up to the performance standard, most of us spend time in neither beautiful states nor states of suffering but end up in a life marked by "OK." We work hard during the weeks and long for the weekend to come. We hope for some extra vacation days and perhaps a pay raise. It becomes a life where we do what we "should" do, the way we "should" do it. Limited by our fear we start compromising with our innermost longing afraid of failure and loss of our perceived value.

Many of us would not like to see fear in ourselves and hide our fear behind words like stress. Think about it, isn´t stress really a code word for fear, more specifically, the fear of what a failure could mean and the feeling of not being enough? In this conversation, it is common for people to say "no, no, no, maybe I'm stressed, but it does not mean that I am afraid to fail. I just have a lot to do." OK, but the question is, why are you stressed about it? Then you might say, "That's just the way it is, some things just have to get done on time..." OK, and if not? "Well, then maybe people will be upset." And what if they get upset? "Yes, but then they will think I have failed." Oh well, so what? "Yes, if they think I have failed, they eventually will question my ability and perhaps even if I'm worthy of the position." "What if they do?" "Then I might get fired." And if you get fired, you will be perceived as a failure and nobody wants to hang around with a failure right?

> *"Stress rooted in the fear of not being enough, which in turn is rooted in the fear of not being loved."*
> –NOAH FROM

The established way to become acknowledged today is through performance. We have to earn our way to recognition. We introduce ourselves with complicated titles, merits and achievements in order to prove our worth. What we are really saying is: "This is what I have done, I have something of value, worthy of your attention".

People´s and society´s praise of materialistic success and achievement have turned failure of attaining it, into our worst nightmare. The fear of failure manifests itself in many ways. To prioritize work over family is one of the most common ways. When it comes to work, we are in control. We learn the rules and deliver tangible results. Raising our children though, is a whole different story. To manage our own feelings while understanding the dynamics of intimate relationships is a place where we many times can feel like falling short. By keeping busy doing things which we know we can deliver on, we avoid feelings and situations that compromise our self-image. Failure means worthless, and who will love somebody who is worthless right? Would we even be capable of loving ourselves if we see ourselves as worthless?

We might live in a time of extraordinary resources, but do we really live extraordinary lives? Divorces, stress, burnouts, sick-leaves, and obesity, could be indicators that we are hungry for something more than just food, money, work, netflix, media, another party, and more action in our lives.

TO FIND HEAVEN IN HELL

Rwanda, in 1994, was hell on earth. About one million people were killed in cold blood genocide. Teachers killed their students, friends gave each other up, and neighbors abused neighboring children. Antonia was one of those who did everything in her power, but still lost her entire family and was subjected to numerous sexual assaults. As a result of the abuse, she became HIV infected and also pregnant with the perpetrator's child. After the war, Antonia experienced a painful hatred, an indescribable despair and a wish to die.

When the war ended and most of the killing might have ended, the aftermath would prove to be ever so painful for Antonia. She was cast out and rejected by the people around her. Nobody wanted to touch someone who had "allowed" herself to be raped. "How can we spend time with a dying widow, that "betrayed" her own family?" people said. Antonia may physically have survived the genocide, but inwardly she felt dead and worthless.

After the war ended, women who shared Antonia's experience, started to gather in small collectives. When Antonia for the first time visited such collective, she suddenly felt an overwhelming sense of hatred against the women of the collective. In retrospect, she understood that her hatred was a desperate cry for help. All she wanted was that someone would rescue her from the swamp of anguish. Her recurrent outbursts were rooted in her fear of starting to feel hope, only to realize that no one or nothing could save her from her unbearable pain. Antonia stayed with the women in the collective. They worked together and lived a simple life. Every day, they would gather, talk and help each other to not get lost in the darkness that so many of them felt on the inside.

When Antonia told me her story, her voice was calm, her eyes soft, and she made me feel safe. She made me understand that her hatred for others was the result of living life at the mercy of circumstances. As long as she held the world responsible for her state, she remained a victim of everything that happened to her, without the ability to change.

Despite her hateful behavior, the women in the community never stopped to show her unconditional love. They introduced a love that never gave up, never stopped believing, that always hoped and love that endured all things. Whatever she did, she was always loved. Experiencing this kind of love, day in and day out resulted in a growing feeling of gratitude. Slowly, but surely and almost magically the feeling of gratitude started to pour out in the form of love for others.

After some time, Antonia herself had become a loving embrace in which newly arrived women could rest. A life of giving, gave Antonia meaning. Love made her discover her potential to overcome her past and her ability to improve the lives of others. She also discovered that she could love just like women of the collective had loved her, unconditionally. Love was a constant power that she had and which no one could take away from her. Today, she shares her story with the ambassadors and representatives who come from all over the world to visit the collective.

The love we are craving the most and what it demands of us will shape our entire life and character. We develop the skills and characteristics that we believe will give us more of that love. Could it be that the quality of your life reflects the quality of love you have encountered?

If our two biggest fears are states of feeling inadequate and not loved, it's not more than logical that our most wanted state consists of the opposite, namely to feel enough and completely loved. In the light of Antonia's story, we understand that our relationship with love reflects our experience of love.

- Either we can be people who demand and depend on receiving love from others.
- Or we can realize that love have already been given to us and it is ours to give

LIFE'S BIGGEST BREAKTHROUGH

Antonia's breakthrough did not come when the women gave her love, it came when she discovered that their love existed within her. Had love been within Antonia all the time? Of course. Despite all that had happened, there was the potential to love, believe, carry, and help others all the time, she just needed someone to show her what it looked like.

> "Love is not something we have to go looking for.
> It is where we come from"
> -MICHAEL BRADLEY

Antonia's story shows us that the key to feel loved, no matter the circumstances, is to realize that the love within us is our true worth. Its value is constant, unchanging and ours to give. Regardless of who or where we are, if we are among farmers or presidents, we always have the ability to love. Our discovery of love changes everything. To realize that we are carrying the one thing that all of humanity yearns for, tends to alter the way we view ourselves and our self-worth. Love is the root of all good. Without it babies cannot grow (suffers weight faltering). Without love our soul will suffocate. Isolated from eachother, we are dying emotionally slowly but surely, which in turn, not seldomly leads to physical death.

If we anchor our value in external things such as jobs, people´s opinion and money, our perceived value will change or disappear whenever these external factors change or disappear. But if we anchor our value in love which is constant, our perceived value will remain constant.

Have you ever felt loved while feeling completely worth-less? Probably not, because it's not possible. Love derives from the feeling of being valuable. As long as Antonia felt worthless or as if she had nothing of value, she suffered from a lack of self-esteem and fear of not being enough and loved. When we discover the love within us, we have also discovered our true value, our power to love unconditionally.

Unconditional love is striving to reach and love people in a way that enables them to discover their own constant value. The women in the community teach us that unconditional love is spelled, "Give without expecting anything in return." Love does not say, "What can I get here?" but rather "What can I give here?"

LIFE´S BIGGEST CHALLANGE COMES WITH THE GREATEST REWARD

To love people unconditionally is probably one of life's greatest challenges and therefore carries life's greatest reward, namely, a wonderful life. To love and to give, no matter how people treat us, challenges us every day to develop our own ability to focus on the good in people who seem to dislike us, give the hopeless situations a meaning that generates hope and learn how to master our emotional states in times of trial. *The miracle behind love is not what it gives us, but what it makes of us as individuals.* The challenge to love unconditionally enables us to grow every day and become people that regardless of circumstances can feel valuable, more than enough, and deeply loved.

The more we discover the value within us, the more value we can provide. The natural result of providing more value is that people perceive us as more valuable. I do not intend to downgrade love to some kind of tool that we strategically use to get what we want, on the other hand, it is good to remember that love is practical, endless, and will create unavoidable results of success in all areas of life where we practice it.

> *"Power based on love is a thousand times more effective and permanent than the one derived from fear of punishment."*
> - GANDHI

The Love that Antonia discovered was a love that had the capacity to take her and others from a state of despair to a life worth living. Similarly, the love inside of us has the power to create purpose and meaning in our lives. The love within us has the power to infuse life into relationships that seem to be over. Love has the capacity to reach into people who seem impossible to reach. Love can and will transform people in our surrounding.

Here comes the most important part of the entire book. The key to Antonia's transformation was that someone showed her unconditional love. Even though she initially hated and spat on the women who tried to help her, they continued to love her. She may not have deserved their love, but unconditional love can not be earned, it is given. Someone who reads this may say, "I have never experienced such unconditional love so how can I give it". Is that true? If we really think about it, we can see that we all have experienced unconditional love. Just put your hands on your heart, feel it beating, as long as it's beats, you're alive. You have not done anything to earn your heart or anything else in your body. Whatever you choose to do with your life, the fact remains that it is an unconditional gift that you have not done a single thing to deserve. Somebody loves you unconditionally.

Personal development and self-discovery are actually a story of the love that lies behind our entire existence. The more we explore our potential and our inner resources, the more we get to experience the unconditional love that has been shown us. The insight about what we have been given unconditionally can result in the same gratitude that Antonia experienced, if we let it. The more we discover this love, the more we can give it and the more we give it, the more we will experience the power of it. It's this way love can be the best of the driving forces. The key to a happy life is that we understand that the first person who must experience our unconditional love is ourselves.

> *"Love your neighbor as yourself*
> – THE BIBLE

Love has mesmerized thinkers for millennia and continues to be an endless mystery. To put your finger on something so complex as love and to put into words something which cannot can be seen as nothing more than a noble effort to define the indefinable. However, history is packed with people who seem to have experienced a love so strong that they have given their lives on the mission to pay it forward. These people help us to recognize real love and to understand further what power lays resting in it.

TAKE AWAYS

Our greatest desire in life is to experience a state of feeling valuable enough and loved as we are. All fear is rooted in two, the fear of:

- Not being enough
- Not being love

When we forget that love is something that can be found within us, we start living a life acquiring outer success in order to deserve love. The quest to become valuable enough to be loved becomes a life where we at the expense of our physical and emotional health are working very hard to maintain our success, status, and reputation. When we get tired, we tend to use external factors to distract us for a while before our thirst for love leads us back to the wheel of performance.

The secret to constant love is the realization that love arises from the feeling of being valuable. We cannot feel loved if we feel worthless. The secret to a wonderful life lies in the realization that we are unconditionally loved and that the same love lies resting within us. It is the love that has been given us that is our true value. No matter who you are, you are carrying the most sought after "commodity" in the world, unconditional love. It is not something we have to perform, it is something that flows naturally the more we receive it.

BONUS

OUR TEN MOST COMMON FEELINGS, WHAT THEY MEAN AND HOW WE CAN HANDLE THEM

All our "negative" feelings carry valuable messages. These messages tell us that we must change either the way we imagine the situation or our way of acting (or both). We have the choice to either stay in our feelings or make use of the message and change the way we feel.

Fear - Means it's time to prepare for something that's expected to happen in the future. Solution: After you have prepared, it is important to tell your brain that you are prepared and move your focus from what you don't want to happen to what you do want in the situation.

Hurt - You experience hurt when one or more of your needs have not been met. It may also mean that you have not met another person's need. The solution is to communicate your needs more clearly or to change the way you are trying to satisfy your or the other persons need.

Anger - Means that your personal rules have been violated. We all have rules on how people and life should be. Most times our anger is the result of violating our own rules and wanting others to take responsibility for it. The solution is to review which one of our rules that are absolutely necessary to have. Fewer rules, less anger.

Frustration - Means that your current approach is not working. You can still succeed, but you have to change your approach.

Disappointment - You expected something to happen but it didn't. The solution is to let it go. Staying disappointed will make you bitter. Do not stay there. Instead, change your state and start focusing on what you do want and take a first small step in that direction.

Guilt - You have broken one of your most important values and did not live up to the standard for your life. The solution is: 1) Review and become aware of your values and what standard you have for your life. Are they reasonable? 2) Do something immediately to ensure you will not do it again.

Helpless or depressed- Means that you're trying to take on your whole life, all at once. You cannot swallow a whole whale in one bite. The solution is to start where you are and re-prioritize. Make a list of what's most important in order for you to start feeling better and start taking the first small step towards completing the first thing on that list. As soon as you complete the first thing on the list you will feel better.

Lonely - Means that you must connect with people. The solution is to change your perception of being alone and go out and meet someone. Volunteer at a local church or a homeless shelter. Start playing sports or join a reading club. Give love to someone. The key is to be able to provide without expecting to get something in return.

Inadequate - Means that you are making unreasonable demands on yourself. The solution is to change the demands or decide to master the area and focus all your resources (time, money, talent) on it. Could you tie your shoes the first time you tried? Of course not, but today you are pretty good at doing it right? How come? Practice.

Unwanted stress - Reveals a destructive way of imagining the situation and a destructive way of using your body. The root of stress is the fear of what a failure might bring. Our brain is designed to survive. If you let it run on autopilot, it will look for anything that can go wrong and magnify it. Five practical steps that you can take to deal with unwanted stress are the following:

1. Stand guard at the door of your mind and feed it only things that build you up. Do not allow weeds to grow. Your current thoughts are the fruit of what you have been planting in your mind through the years.
2. Strengthen your body. The state of fear is physical. Research shows that physical activity activates your biochemistry and allows your body and mind to work more efficiently together.
3. Find a mission that is greater than yourself, your pain and your joy. Become part of something bigger that inspires you.
4. Find a role model, someone who has done what you want to do. It will give you a sense of hope and belief that the same thing is possible for you.
5. Help someone else. To help someone who is going through an even tougher time than yourself will put your life in perspective. No matter how bad it looks for you, you can always help someone else. Your ability to give and help will contribute to community and give you the power to try again and move on.

EPILOGUE

Welcome to the end of the book. Thank you for coming on this "emotional" journey. My goal has been for you and I to discover and understand one of life's most powerful resource, our feelings. Since feelings are invisible, many people tend to miss or do not give priority to learning or understanding how to make use of them. What could be more unfortunate than miss out on learning and understanding the power that controls all of our decisions and our well-being?

The prerequisite for us to be able to live a wonderful life and a life of complete freedom is to take full responsibility for our feelings and not become slaves to circumstances and other people's actions.

We have now acquired the basics of how we can live a wonderful life. Now I want to challenge you to slowly, but surely begin to translate the content of this book in practice. What we talked about in this book is a lifelong journey. The key to discover what we have been given on the inside is to remember the following three things:

- Since life is not about getting but becoming, we cannot fail. Nelson Mandela once said, "I never lose, I either win or learn."

- When we feel like we are not achieving what we want, it is important to remember to thank ourselves for the courage it takes to tackle life's greatest challenge: Know Thyself

- Be grateful for the challenges life brings you. They will help you to discover your God-given potential and enable you to grow and become more of who you truly are.

Let us now join the people who have gone before us. The people who did not settle for survival and mere existence, but learned to utilize their feelings to design a wonderful life. Let us become WONDERFEEL

/ NOAH FROM

EXPLORE YOUR POTENTIAL

&

LIVE TO GROW

For more resources and contact:
www.noahfrom.com

PS:

IF YOU CAN`T GET ENOUGH

For those of you who are "hooked on a feeling" I want offer a simple excercise, which you can do together with your friends, team or family. This will help you to find out where you live currently, emotionally. When we know where we live, we can choose if we want to keep on living there or if we want to build a new emotional home, which will far more strenghtening. A Wonderfeel home.

<u>*This is how we identify and build a WONDERFEEL home.*</u>

1. Grab a pen and use an empty page in the back of this book and make two columns. Above the one column, write "wonderful feelings" and above the other "unwanted feelings."

2. Now, take 5 minutes and write down all the feelings that you experience during a week under each column. This will show you what your current residence looks like.

3. When you have written down your feelings, I want you to look under the column "unwanted feelings" and select the two most common unwanted feelings that you experience during a normal week.

4. Time to find the cure. The cure to an unwanted feeling is always the opposite feeling. Simply put, if you are sad, the cure is most likely joy or if you are afraid, the cure is most likely courage. Find the cure that you consider to be the opposite.

5. Select one of the cure feelings. Now I want you to remember a time when you experienced that wonderful feeling. When you have found the memory, ask yourself the following questions: "How did I use my body at that point? What did I focus on? What meaning did I give the situation? How did I act?

6. When you clearly see how you used your physiology and what you focused on to experience the wonderful feeling, it's time to start training and build a highway to that emotional state.

7. Throughout the coming week, every time you experience the unwanted feeling, remember how you used your body and your focus. Then, recreate the same radical change in your body and focus on the same thing.

This will be your map to wonderful states, and you already have the resources to build your dream home. I heard a carpenter say, "It's simple to build a house, but it is not easy." To build a new emotional home requires time and energy. Life is about building a house in which we can stay even when it storms, rains, and snows, so let's start building it today.